# A Faithful Presence

## Working Together for the Common Good

Hilary Russell

scm press

© Hilary Russell 2015

Published in 2015 by SCM Press
Editorial office
3rd Floor
Invicta House
108-114 Golden Lane
London
EC1Y 0TG

SCM Press is an imprint of Hymns Ancient & Modern Ltd (a registered charity)
13A Hellesdon Park Road
Norwich NR6 5DR, UK

www.scmpress.co.uk

Scripture quotations are from the New Revised Standard Version of the Bible,
Anglicized Edition, copyright © 1989, 1995 by the Division of Christian
Education of the National Council of the Churches of Christ in the USA. Used
by permission. All rights reserved.

'For God's Sake Let Us Dare' by Elizabeth Cosnett is used by permission of
Stainer & Bell.

British Library Cataloguing in Publication data

A catalogue record for this book is available
from the British Library

9780334053897

Typeset by Mary Matthews
Printed and bound by
CPI Group (UK) Ltd

# Contents

# Acknowledgements

There are many people to thank for their support in the preparation of this book. It would not have been written at all had it not been for the Together for the Common Good (T4CG) initiative, which was the brainchild of Jenny Sinclair. I am particularly grateful to Jenny and to other members of the T4CG steering group for their ongoing encouragement and trust, especially as they did not know what I might be hatching. In the book, I have drawn on the T4CG research that was done in 2013, and I want to thank my colleague Dr Gerwyn Jones, who conducted most of the fieldwork interviews, and all those who agreed to be interviewed and share their experience and expertise. Some have been quoted and named – with their permission – in the book, but many others took part and all the material gathered was very valuable.

In a less direct way, many of the projects and stories cited here – and the people associated with them – have been personally formative for me. These have included my involvement in:

- Merseyside Churches Urban Institute, which was sponsored by Bishop David Sheppard, Archbishop Derek Worlock, the Revd Dr John Newton and the then Vice Chancellor of University of Liverpool, Professor Sir Graeme Davies.
- Church Action on Poverty, especially during my close connection in the late 1980s and 1990.
- Merseyside and Region Churches Ecumenical Assembly – now Churches Together in the Merseyside Region.

- Together Liverpool, the joint venture between Liverpool Diocese and the Church Urban Fund and, linked with that, the Together Network.

A number of people have read sections of the book in draft, and I am most grateful to them: Andrew Bradstock, Bob Fyfe, Kevin Kelly and Colin Marsh. Thanks too to Dave Walker for allowing me to use his cartoons. Finally, I am deeply indebted to Natalie Watson, senior commissioning editor of SCM Press, for her sustained encouragement and guidance. However, the views expressed and any weaknesses within the book are all my own.

# 1
# Beginnings

*[T]he Church represented an enduring, faithful presence ... so that the flux and uncertainty all around could be more bravely confronted ... In effect, the churches stood for an alternative way of life to that of the individualism and materialism which threatened our survival as a human society.*

Don May and Margaret Simey 1989

What is the purpose of this short book? The impetus for it was to bring together and explore some of the themes underpinning the Together for the Common Good (T4CG) initiative. However, insofar as these reflect themes that have lingered with me over the past several decades, the book has a more personal flavour than originally intended. And because I have lived here for nearly all my adult life, the Liverpool context has very much informed my experience and thinking.

## Scouse roots

Together for the Common Good began from the idea that there was still something to be learnt from the partnership of the church leaders here on Merseyside from the 1970s through to the 1990s, when the Roman Catholic Archbishop Derek Worlock, the Anglican Bishop of Liverpool David Sheppard and their Free Church colleagues, such as John Williamson, Keith Hobbs and Eric Allen and especially John Newton, worked so closely together.

1

Liverpool then was a very different place religiously, politically, socially and economically; and, as all cities are distinctive, it was different from other cities in England. Although sectarian tension between Protestants and Catholics was already on the wane, there were other social and economic pressures. Steep rates of poverty stemmed from, and were accompanied by, other problems. Unemployment was high. A lot of the housing in the city and surrounding areas was in poor condition. Population loss as the better qualified moved out in search of more promising opportunities meant growing disparity between income from rates and the city's infrastructure costs. Although many members of the black community had roots in the city over several generations, they remained on the fringe of the social and economic mainstream. A succession of minority and coalition administrations over the 1970s and early 1980s meant a lack of strategic direction in the City Council. When the Militant Tendency came to power, the determined clash between local and central government further worsened the city's reputation, deterred investors and distracted from properly serving the interests of residents and businesses. There were faults on both sides. On the one hand, the council exploited the city's problems as part of a wider political agenda. On the other, the government's punitive grant system made claims of unfair treatment persuasive and 'even the Government's own Audit Commission delivered a withering attack on the unpredictability and irrationality of the system which wholly reinforced Liverpool's arguments' (Parkinson 1985, p. 176).

Liverpool at that time, therefore, desperately needed advocates and bridge builders, and it found them in these church leaders. They set aside what might have divided them in church terms to concentrate on what united them. Theirs was not a navel-gazing, inward-looking ecumenism focusing on the finer points of theological difference and negotiating institutional interest, rather it was an ecumenism of kingdom building. They wanted to bring practical improvements to people's lives and to local neighbourhoods. And through their 'better together' ministry, they brought a gospel that really spoke to people, especially those who were disadvantaged and marginalized.

## Reflection, conversation …

Reflection and action for change are complementary aspects of what T4CG is about. It is not just retrospective. It has become a growing movement of people and organizations interested in building commitment to the flourishing of all and exploring what this might mean and how it might be achieved in today's social, economic and political circumstances. One focus is on engaging with people in a position to bring about change and who are open to collaborating with others to address social problems.

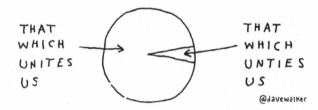

But it was also always intended that the initiative should result in different sorts of written materials and other tools for analysing the present-day context and exploring how different traditions of Christian thought can enlighten our search for social justice today. The website – www.togetherforthecommongood.com – lists resources and contains a range of opinion pieces and case studies.

An important book was published in 2015, *Together for the Common Good: Towards a National Conversation*, edited by

Nicholas Sagovsky and Peter McGrail. Accompanied by a study guide, this assembles essays by academics, politicians and others contributing very varied perspectives on the common good, mainly from different Christian denominations and traditions but also including Jewish, Muslim and secular contributions and spanning different political perspectives. The word 'conversation' in the title is significant. Conversations took place among the contributors during the time they were writing, and the essays themselves are intended to prompt further conversations. The book's timing was significant, coming as it did a few months before the General Election.

> True godliness don't turn men out of the world but enables them to live better in it and excites their endeavours to mend it. Christians should keep the helm and guide the vessel to its port; not meanly steal out at the stern of the world and leave those that are in it without a pilot to be driven by the fury of evil times upon the rock or sand of ruin.
>
> William Penn 1682

Whether in the creation of manifestos or in the decisions of electors about how to cast their votes, elections always pose questions about reconciling self-interest and the common good. But in a time when politics often seem dominated by management-speak, the pertinence of reawakening debate on principles and values is not confined to the run-up to elections, rather it has to be part of a longer-term attempt to change the terms of the debate and move towards re-imagining politics.

## ... and action

The essays in *Together for the Common Good* represent attempts to interpret the world today from a UK standpoint. But the imperative behind the book is the need for action: action based on clear-eyed recognition of the reality facing us and wise judgement about a good way forward.

> To say this is to say something about the quality of 'conversation' which must take place before there can be well-judged action which serves the common good. Conversation of this quality must be patient, attentive, well-informed and robust. It must be rooted in the needs and experience of local communities. It must be rooted in action and lead to action. Conversation of this quality is intended to change the world, in a transformative way to serve the common good. (Sagovsky and McGrail 2015, p. xviii)

*Together for the Common Good* primarily addresses the 'common good' part of T4CG. This present book focuses more upon the 'together' dimension, the relationships that can foster or inhibit joint working towards the common good. It draws in part on research that I led prior to and immediately following the T4CG conference in 2013, which included a large number of fieldwork interviews conducted by Gerwyn Jones of the European Institute for Urban Affairs, Liverpool John Moores University. This book has been informed by the research findings and includes quotes – with their permission – from some of the interviewees.

I take for granted that faith encompasses social action. It can take many forms: opening up the Church to the local community, taking part in neighbourhood projects, volunteering in a foodbank, spending time cleaning up the environment, sleeping out to raise funds for a homeless charity, or supporting social justice campaigns – the list is endless. But 'social action' is not something that can be boxed off; not a particular brand of Christian witness confined only to people with certain callings or inclinations, rather it encompasses our ways of living in the world. And as such it takes us beyond one-to-one relationships – though, of course, these too are 'social' – to our role in wider society.

## Engagement towards transformation

Given that David Sheppard and Derek Worlock largely inspired T4CG, it is serendipitous that 2015 marks two anniversaries separately linked with them. First, it is 50 years this year since the end of the Second Vatican Council, which was such a major event in the history of the Roman Catholic Church. Vatican II took place at an influential time in Archbishop Derek Worlock's formation, and he attended as Secretary to Cardinal William Godfrey. Second, in December 2015 it will be 30 years since the publication of *Faith in the City*, the report of the Archbishop of Canterbury's Commission on Urban Priority Areas, of which Bishop David Sheppard was vice chair. Both in different ways were landmarks. Vatican II was concerned with the fitness of the Roman Catholic Church for its engagement in today's world. The purpose of the Council was to equip the Church to transform the modern world, though this was sometimes mistakenly interpreted as 'adapting the Church to the modern world by making it more like the modern world' (Ivereigh 2014, p. 90). *Faith in the City* was prompted by what was happening in England's inner cities and on outer housing estates. Concern that had been mounting for some time was brought to a head by the disorders in different cities in the summer of 1981 and again in 1985. The report raised questions about the impact of public policies on urban priority areas (UPAs) but it also drew attention to aspects of church life that were seen as a recipe for alienation between the Church of England and people living in UPAs. The dual focus was important: 'Only when the church is serious about setting its own house in order can it call on the state to do justly and love mercy' (Forrester 1989, p. 86).

What does it mean for Christians and the Church to 'do justly, and to love mercy' (Micah 6.8 KJV) and to have the integrity to call on others to do likewise? The rest of this book seeks to examine these questions. Chapter 2 continues this introductory section by giving a brief introduction to the common good. The following four chapters look at different dimensions of how Christians pursue the common good and the nature of their collaboration: trends in ecumenism today, aspects of church involvement in the world, examples of social action and the task of speaking out in public life. The final chapter brings together the various threads and poses questions that I hope might continue this 'conversation'.

# 2
# Common Good:
# Conversation and Transformation

## A current concern

*Although Christian teaching can give no policy prescriptions, it can provide values and principles to guide us as well as giving the motive force for change. The concept of the common good is closely linked with that of social justice. It has been especially prominent in Roman Catholic teaching ... Such a guiding concept is clearly open to differing interpretations and its application must inevitably be modified in relation to historical and cultural circumstances. [But] it articulates a challenge which must always be faced.*

Hilary Russell 1995, pp. 264–5

Since I wrote that passage 20 years ago, the idea of the common good has come into much wider use and not just among Roman Catholics or even just among Christians. The idea of the common good extends beyond faith groups to secular bodies. Wherever and whenever people are critical of the status quo and searching for alternatives, they need some binding concept that can help shape their vision and frame their thinking. A recent example was when, in 2013, a group of civil society organizations sent out a Call to Action for the Common Good addressed to the voluntary, public and private sectors and proposed a national debate to stimulate people to apply the principles within their organizations and within their sphere of influence. It came out of a wish to develop a more hopeful national story of change to address many of the big challenges faced across the country. Two seminars and a report followed in 2014. It continued to engage change makers across the sectors in order to define common good principles more sharply and find practical applications.

Steve Wyler asks what it would mean to work together for the common good. It is not simply a matter of combining common sense and good management to tackle a shared problem, or of better co-operation, reducing 'silo' working or building alliances. Vested interests, inertia and obstruction all make it more difficult. And there are hard questions about who decides priorities, how people with conflicting interests can work together and who will be included.

> Can common good be accomplished from on high, or does it require a local people-sized community approach? The common good reveals itself as something which must be deeply contested, subjected to deliberative debate, if it is to mean anything worthwhile. (Wyler 2014, p. 41)

However, when people do work together for the common good it can be intensely liberating.

> Power and ownership and risk and reward are distributed more widely, trust and friendships are built, new forms of solidarity emerge. And at the centre of this, as Catholic social teaching asserts, is always the quality of relationships between people and the commitments they are prepared to make to each other. Like myself, you don't have to be a Catholic, or religious at all, to realize that this could be quite important. (Wyler 2014, p. 41)

This secular view underlines that the common good does not happen of itself, rather it has to be made and continually remade and is not something that can be imposed by an elite, however

9

well-meaning. How then can people-powered change be brought about? This chapter seeks to explore some of the concepts that underpin the idea of the common good; subsequent ones examine ways it may be pursued.

## What are the key ingredients of the common good?

> *The common good challenges us to address the fundamental, and essentially religious, question of what it means to be human. It asks whether we primarily see ourselves as autonomous individuals, whose goal as a society extends only as far as realizing individual potential, individual goals and individual freedom, free from any responsibility to seek a common purpose or care for those unable to realize these individual goals? Or whether we believe that our humanity is constituted most profoundly by our relationships, such that our personal wellbeing includes reference to the fact of our sharing a common life together.*
>
> Andrew Bradstock, in Sagovsky and McGrail 2015, p. 27

There is always a danger of the term 'common good' being used in such a general and abstract 'motherhood and apple pie' way that it is emptied of any real meaning. Catholic Social Teaching – sometimes referred to as 'Catholic Social Thought', though I shall use the 'Teaching' form in this book – provides the starting point for common-good thinking. Although the roots go back much further, the Catholic Church has reiterated themes on the social dimension of Christ's teaching since the late nineteenth century. *Gaudium et spes* (1965) defines the common good as 'the sum total of social conditions which allow people, either as groups or as individuals, to reach their fulfilment more fully and more easily' (paragraph 26). The human person achieves his or her potential as a member of society, and the increasing interdependence between 'the betterment of the person and the improvement of society' brought about by modern life makes the role of the common good more important. Not only do individuals and groups have to set their own interests in the context of the good of all, therefore, but also governments and other institutions have to safeguard and promote the common good.

## Human dignity

From the perspective of Catholic Social Teaching and all biblical teaching, every human being is infinitely valuable and loved in the eyes of God, regardless of ethnicity, gender, religion or physical appearance. In other words, this is a recognition that, in Rowan Williams' words:

> every person is related to God before they are related to anything or anyone else; that God has defined who they are and who they can be by his own eternal purpose ... This means that whenever I face another human being, I face a mystery ... I stand on holy ground when I encounter another person. (Williams 2007)

This is why a Christian understanding of human dignity encompasses but also goes beyond a commitment to the legal entitlement of all to human rights. It rests upon an underlying reverence:

> The reverence I owe to every human person is connected with the reverence I owe to God's creative word, which brings them into being and keeps them in being ... It means that there are no superfluous people, no 'spare' people in the human world. All are needed for the good of all. (Williams 2007)

Pope John Paul II put it that 'the 'dignity of the human person is a transcendent value'. To 'promote the good of the individual is thus to serve the common good, which is that point where rights

> *It means therefore that a human person is worth extravagant and lasting commitment. A human person deserves complete attention and care, whether rich or poor, whether they will live for a day or for six decades.*
>
> Rowan Williams 2007

and duties converge and reinforce one another' (John Paul II, 'Message for the 1999 World Day of Peace', paragraph 2).

In 1965, Vatican II developed the implications of this and spoke of the 'growing awareness of the sublime dignity of human persons, whose rights and duties are universal and inviolable. They ought, therefore, to have ready access to all that is necessary for living a genuinely human life.' All people have a right and a duty to participate in the economic, political and cultural life of society and should be assured of that right. Human dignity requires it; justice demands it. The common good cannot be promoted or achieved without that participation, making it fundamentally wrong to exclude any person or group from participating, at least minimally, in society. Interestingly this idea of exclusion is close to Peter Townsend's definition of people being in poverty when they lack the resources to obtain the type of diet, participate in the activities and have the living conditions that are customary in their society.

> *Every day human interdependence grows more tightly drawn and spreads by degrees over the whole world. As a result the common good, that is, the sum of those conditions of social life which allow social groups and their individual members relatively thorough and ready access to their own fulfilment, today takes on an increasingly universal complexion and consequently involves rights and duties with respect to the whole human race. Every social group must take account of the needs and legitimate aspirations of other groups, and even of the general welfare of the entire human family.*
>
> Gaudium et spes, para 26

These understandings of human dignity, therefore, highlight interdependence and mutual care. However, they also signal the importance of human agency. In our concern for others, we need to guard against any distinction between the do-ers and the done-to. Self-fulfilment requires taking responsibility and being answerable for oneself. This is relevant not only to interpersonal relationships but also to the relationships that form the fabric of our society: at all levels and in all circumstances, not only between the state and the individuals but in all 'those networks in which negotiation – the shaping together of human dignity – actually happens' (Williams 2008, p. 2).

> *Human dignity is threatened in our domestic society by poverty and injustice of whatever kind.*
> Catholic Bishops' Conference 1980, paragraph 174

Defenders of the welfare state will often baulk at criticisms that suggest it represents a 'nanny state' or creates a dependency culture. Such criticisms frequently assume that dependency is a bad thing and ignore the extent to which we are all necessarily – and thankfully – dependent in one way or another. However, a stress on the need to acknowledge personal agency is a useful counterbalance to the danger of providing welfare in a way that confines rather than enlarges the horizons of the individual: 'Welfare is about releasing the self for well-being, to shape and discover that well-being with other selves and other agents' (Williams 2008, p. 2). As a principle, this can be a yardstick for considering how best, for example, to frame social security systems or administer health and social care.

## Solidarity

As well as personal interdependence, human society can be viewed as a 'community of communities', a set of interlinking communities – family, neighbourhood, town, national and international. Two principles of Catholic Social Teaching refer to the way these different communities interrelate horizontally (solidarity) and vertically (subsidiarity).

*Vote for the Common Good*, the pamphlet issued by the Catholic Bishops' Conference in anticipation of the 2001 General Election, says that solidarity – awareness of our shared humanity – lies at the heart of the notion of the common good.

> *Solidarity is first and foremost a sense of responsibility on the part of everyone with regard to everyone.*
> Pope Benedict XVI, 2009, paragraph 38

The notion of solidarity flows naturally from the value placed upon human dignity and recognition of the personal and societal responsibility associated with our interconnectedness.

> [It] is not a feeling of vague compassion or shallow distress at the misfortunes of so many people, both near and far. On the contrary, it is a firm and persevering determination to commit oneself to the common good; that is to say, to the good of all and of each individual, because we are all really responsible for all. (Pope John Paul II 1987, paragraph 38)

> *[C]ommon good is more like an activity, a set of responsibilities or a common project, which is inconceivable when individuals are thought about as isolated one from another.*
> Esther Reed, in Sagovsky and McGrail 2015, p. 58

Pope Francis (2014) has said that:

> The many situations of inequality, poverty and injustice, are signs not only of a profound lack of fraternity, but also of the absence of a culture of solidarity. New ideologies, characterized by rampant individualism, egocentrism and materialistic consumerism, weaken social bonds, fuelling

that 'throw away' mentality which leads to contempt for, and the abandonment of, the weakest and those considered 'useless'.

> *We Christians aspire to an unimaginable solidarity that is not against anyone. It is not based on exclusion, of an 'us' against 'them'. The kingdom is solidarity without exclusion, offering us an identity beyond our present understanding. Until the kingdom, we are incomplete people. It is not only the poor, the powerless and the voiceless who lack full identity. We do, too, until we are one with them.*
>
> Timothy Radcliffe, quoted in *live*simply 2013, p. 143

Solidarity crosses continents, especially in this age of rapid communication when we can be instantly aware of wars, famines and floods on the other side of the world and especially in our ever more interconnected world when the consequences of our way of life for others are all too discernible. Solidarity also crosses generations, allowing or encouraging us to feel responsibility for the past and for the future, whether looking back at the consequences of the actions of our own or past generations or

> *There is a world of difference between praying for rather than with the poor.*
>
> John Battle, undated

looking forward to the potential consequences for our children and grandchildren of our profligate use of the world's resources.

## Subsidiarity

The principle of subsidiarity is that nothing should be done by a larger and more complex body if it can be done by a smaller and simpler one. Subsidiarity as a term came into more prominent use through the 1992 Maastricht Treaty. Although it had featured earlier in relation to some European Union policy spheres, this treaty enshrined the principle of subsidiarity – that matters should be dealt with at the lowest possible level – as fundamental to European decision-making. Central, high-level authorities should only perform those tasks that cannot be carried out more locally and they have a duty to ensure local groups have the requisite freedom and capacity to act. The purpose was to protect the powers of member states but also to ensure that powers are exercised as closely to the citizen as possible.

> *Basic justice demands the establishment of minimum levels of participation in the life of the human community for all persons. The ultimate injustice is for a person or group to be treated actively or abandoned passively as if they were nonmembers of the human race. To treat people this way is effectively to say that they simply do not count as human beings.*
>
> United States Catholic Bishops 1986, p. 18

The example of the European Union illustrates that the application of the principle of subsidiarity is always likely to be controversial. Deciding the appropriate level of decision-making will invariably be open to dispute, and conclusions will change according to changing circumstances. Although most often the pressure needs to be towards lower- rather than higher-level powers, some roles must necessarily be performed by the state – they cannot be further delegated. Similarly, in a world where nation states can give only limited protection to their citizens against economic storms, social disruption or environmental damage across the globe, the balance of argument may shift towards more international agreement on policies and practices.

At the start of her 2002 Reith Lectures, *A Question of Trust*, Onora O'Neill quotes Confucius saying that three things are needed for government: weapons, food and trust, and the one a ruler should hold on to most firmly is trust. Trust is essential to individuals and institutions. Consciously or unconsciously, we use trust as a criterion for what we do and say. Trust is the issue that lurks behind concern about the apparently failing health of electoral democracy. Trust is a prerequisite for the development of mechanisms for participative democracy. Arguably, apart from its material impact, the worst consequence of the 2008 credit crisis was the way it undermined trust in major financial institutions. Since then, trust has been further damaged by a sense that the effects of the austerity measures deemed necessary for recovery were predictably uneven and have eroded fairness.

> The removal of intermediate institutions, whether public institutions or as levels of management in organisations of any kind, reduces the opportunity for personal interaction which lies at the heart of trust, of individual satisfaction, and of the possibility of empirically-based improvements in policies of many kinds. Instead we have only economic policies and welfare policies based on doctrine.
>
> Judith Marquand 2013

Local participation extending to each individual is essential to subsidiarity. Although decision-making has to take place at a higher level, it is nevertheless important that individuals feel they can make a difference. Richard Sennett talks about people being excluded from the decisions affecting their own well-being: 'They were rendered spectators to their own needs, mere consumers of care provided to them. It was here that they experienced that peculiar lack of respect that consists of not being seen, not being accounted as full human beings' (Sennett 2003, p. 13).

Austin Smith, a Passionist priest based for many years in Liverpool 8, made a similar observation: 'One of the most radical disadvantages suffered by the powerless and marginalized of our society is their ultimate exclusion from the *conversation* which creates society' (1990, p. 132).

Writing this book in the run-up to the 2015 General Election, the television news repeatedly gives interviews with people who say 'I won't be voting because it makes no difference.' Notably, attitudes are different among those who have been involved in any sort of action in their local area, such as campaigning to keep their children's centre or library open. Representative democracy – and putting an X in a box every few years – is not sufficient. There have to be accompanying opportunities for participative democracy. This requires intermediate levels where groups and individuals can engage.

One of the lessons from community-based regeneration initiatives, however, is that even a 'local people-sized community approach' is far from simple and will still encounter diverse interests, prejudices and attempts to hold on to levers of power and influence. Looking at the sorts of negotiations that occur at neighbourhood level points to factors that are more generally relevant: the importance of personal relationships and building trust; the

> [H]uman wellbeing is about agency – being able to exercise the appropriate, the possible, the fulfilling levels of agency that you can, along with others whose free agency you likewise want to affirm.
> Rowan Williams 2008, p. 3

significance of personal and local histories and of individual and community stories; the need to overcome suspicion and lack of self-confidence. For this we require arenas in which encounter and exchange can take place and bridging organizations in which people can feel their involvement is making a difference. Yet the past 30 to 40 years in the UK have seen the weakening of some institutions that served as such bridges. The hollowing out of local government has been accompanied by a shift from providing space and scope for 'citizens' to providing choice for 'consumers' – a cultural shift that encourages individualism rather than community.

## Option for the poor

Individualism stands in contradiction to an option for the poor or, as David Sheppard called it, a 'bias to the poor'. This option or bias means assessing lifestyles, policies and social institutions in terms of their impact on the most vulnerable and creating conditions for marginalized voices to be heard.

The liberation theologian Gustavo Gutiérrez highlighted how the Old and New Testaments speak of God's preferential love and care for the poor, who have no one else to care for them. The test of a just society is how it treats its most vulnerable members. God's covenant with Israel was dependent on the way the community treated the poor and unprotected – the widow, the orphan and the stranger (see for example Deuteronomy 16.11–12; Exodus 22.21–27; Isaiah 1.7–17). Jesus came to bring good news to the poor (Luke 4.14–21). We are to be judged by how we respond to the hungry, the thirsty, the prisoner, and the stranger (Matthew 25.31–46).

> *The option for the poor ... means taking up the cause of the poor and oppressed in ways which respect them as agents of their own liberation.*
> John Battle, undated

> *Bias to the poor sounds like a statement of political preference. My experience has been that some of the most central teachings of orthodox Christianity lead me to this position. I shall argue from Jesus' theme of the Kingdom of God, the calling of the Church to be Catholic, reaching across all human divisions and the doctrine of the Incarnation; they lead me to claim that there is a divine bias to the poor, which should be reflected both in the Church and in the secular world.*
> David Sheppard 1983, p. 10

> Religion is always personal, but never just a private affair.
> Cardinal Basil Hume 1996, p. 2

This preferential love, as seen in Christ's ministry and teaching, is essential to the preaching of the gospel in every age and must be foundational to the life of the Church.

Pope John Paul II spoke about the option for the poor in *Sollicitudo rei socialis*:

> This is an option, or a special form of primacy in the exercise of Christian charity, to which the whole tradition of the Church bears witness. It affects the life of each Christian inasmuch as he or she seeks to imitate the life of Christ, but it applies equally to our social responsibilities and hence to our manner of living, and to the logical decisions to be made concerning the ownership and use of goods.

> *It is quite scandalous that such a term as 'fundamental option for the poor' should be a theologically debated topic: in terms of the hopefulness of the Kingdom of God, there is not option of any kind, let alone a fundamental one. For the Christian there is simply no choice in the matter, a confrontation with evil and the identification and purging of it are at the heart of the human and Christian journey. But the purgation does not apply only to my personal journey: it is an obligation to be honoured with regard to the ideologies and structures of this world and especially so when such ideologies and structures oppress, alienate and stigmatise the powerless.*
> Austin Smith 1990, p. 126

## Signposts not a blueprint

In 1996 the Catholic Bishops' Conference of England and Wales published a statement, *The Common Good and the Catholic Church's Social Teaching*. Written in the months preceding the 1997 General Election and at a time when many Christian organizations were seeking a change in political direction, the statement strove to make clear that it was not presenting a party political programme, rather it was based on the belief that whereas the Church's social teaching 'provides a set of consistent and complementary principles, values and goals', the best way to achieve these would always be open to debate. In other words, it was a set of signposts, not a blueprint. Nor, the Statement said, are the ideas behind

> *Experience teaches that not all Christians respond in identical fashion when gospel values, which are honoured in the abstract, are applied to specific situations.*
> Catholic Bishops' Conference 1980, paragraph 159

Catholic Social Teaching solely Catholic property. To the extent that they are based on natural law and natural justice using human reason, they are open to anyone. Insofar as Catholic Social Teaching following Vatican II became more Christ-centred and thus more person-centred, these ideas can span the insights of other Christians.

The Church of England's House of Bishops wrote a letter addressed to their people and parishes for the 2015 General Election. It was not a shopping list of policies, rather a call for a new direction for political life. Titled *Who is my Neighbour?*, it also invited all, whether or not they have any church allegiance, to join in the conversation. In addition to identifying specific areas of local, national and international life that call for a renewed political vision and the application of key values in order for 'politics to rise above its present diminished state', the letter recalled the debate on the common good in the July 2014 General Synod. This diagnosed some crucial points:

- Acknowledging the depth of insecurity and anxiety that has permeated our society after decades of rapid change, not least the changes brought about by the banking crisis and austerity programme.

- Recognizing people's need for supportive local communities and that the informal and voluntary sectors hold society together in ways which neither the state nor private enterprise can match.
- Recognizing that people need a sense of place and of belonging.
- Addressing the culture of regulation and litigation when it operates as a 'chill factor' on voluntary involvement, where anxiety about potential litigation can be a brake on local action.
- Reflecting the obligation to secure the common good of future generations, not just our own, and addressing issues of intergenerational justice. This must include a responsible approach to environmental issues.

The application of the common good can help towards more informed political choices and provide a 'vocabulary' to articulate the principles underpinning these choices. It will be controversial. There will be difficulty in establishing facts; differences of analysis and in interpretation of what is politically feasible and desirable. And because the teaching inevitably reflects the reading of circumstances at the time of writing, it means that it must always be kept under review; it cannot be inherited uncritically. Such a task requires the Church not only to draw upon a range of academic disciplines and learn from its experience of day-to-day ministry

> *Whatever is true, whatever is honourable, whatever is just, whatever is pure, whatever is pleasing, whatever is commendable, if there is any excellence and if there is anything worthy of praise, think about these things.*
>
> Philippians 4.8 used as the motif in *Who is my Neighbour?*

but also to mine the riches of different Christian traditions. The next chapter, therefore, looks at where our ecumenical journey is taking us today.

# 3
# 'More Together, Less Apart':
# Ecumenism Today

*Churches should act together in all matters except those in which deep differences of conviction compel them to act separately.*

Lund principle

Christian churches all have the same basic calling: to worship God, to share the good news about Jesus Christ and to work for the good of all people. A main message in this book is that our response to this calling is best undertaken together; this chapter looks briefly at how our understanding of 'better together' is evolving.

> The point of the Ecumenical Movement is that unity and renewal go together. Complacency about the past, and blindness to deficiencies in the present, is no basis for church unity. That is one reason why a soundly-based social theology and witness is so important. It is essential to a renewal of the churches.
>
> Ronald Preston 1994, p. 6

## 'Don't talk about ecumenism'

In 1951 the World Council of Churches said that the ecumenical movement is concerned with the church as a whole and the wholeness of the Church: 'The whole task of the whole church to bring the gospel to the whole world' (quoted in Preston 1994, p. 5). In this context 'wholeness' means both the unity *and renewal* of the churches.

It is sometimes suggested that 'ecumenism' is almost a toxic label or brand nowadays. Certainly there is a sense in which the ecumenical movement has seemed to have become tired – perhaps too focused on structures and organizational formulas.

> *Being Churches Together means commitment by each church and denomination to deepen its fellowship with the others and, without losing what makes each interestingly different, to work with them towards a greater visible unity.*
>
> Churches Together in Britain and Ireland (CTBI) website

Yet it is called a 'movement', which implies that to be healthy it requires dynamism and responsiveness to change. And looking more closely, many such signs of vibrancy and vigour are discernible. Ecumenism lives on in different forms and guises, even if not labelled as such.

There have long been ecumenical structures, not just regionally and locally through Churches Together groups but also:

- Internationally: the World Council of Churches (WCC).
- Nationally for each of the four nations: CYTUN (Churches Together in Wales); Action for Churches Together in Scotland (ACTS); the Irish Council of Churches; Churches Together in England (CTE);
- For Britain and Ireland: Churches Together in Britain and Ireland (CTBI).

The ecumenical movement has traditionally described twin strands of potential unity: faith and order; life and work. Of course, work continues towards the first strand of unity. In its first major publication since *Baptism, Eucharist and Ministry* in 1982, the WCC Commission on Faith and Order produced *The Church: Towards a Common Vision* in 2012. As the fruit of many years of work on ecclesiology by representative theologians from Orthodox, Anglican, Protestant, Evangelical, Pentecostal and Roman Catholic churches, it asks what can be said together about the Church and how closer mutual understanding might contribute to overcoming the obstacles standing in the way of unity between the divided Christian communities. It was sent to member churches to encourage reflection and seek responses. The foreword by Olav Fykse Tveit, the WCC General Secretary, stresses the inseparability of the two strands when he says that '[w]ork on ecclesiology relates to everything the Church is and what its mission implies in and for the world'.

Increasingly, however, the focus seems to be on life and work. In Britain the shift has been away from what might be seen as a rather static preoccupation with 'structural' ecumenism, and away from 'doing ecumenical things' or 'calendar ecumenism', towards the more active interpretation of 'doing things ecumenically'. This is perhaps a braver and more adult ecumenism, which is not afraid of the different histories and different cultures in different churches but rather seeks to take advantage of their collective riches.

## Belonging inextricably together

'More together, less apart' is the strapline of CTBI. But before considering some examples of 'doing things ecumenically' in later chapters, it is worth looking at the changing context and some of the drivers that influence the current approach. There has always been a measure of resistance to searching for unity: sometimes a weariness induced by repeatedly coming across doctrinal brick walls; sometimes a more pervasive reluctance to contemplate change. For those for whom 'the church as they know it is a rock of stability to them in a disturbing and changing world' (Preston 1994, p. 6), renewal may be too challenging. But it may also be that past approaches were stultifying; that they seemed far removed from active discipleship and making a difference in the world. Dame Mary Tanner was the first General Secretary of the Church of England Council for Christian Unity and former European President of the World Council of Churches. At the Together for the Common Good conference in September 2013 she asked why much of the passion for Christian unity has evaporated.

Is it because we advocates of the 70s, 80s and 90s made it seem as if Christian unity was a sort of end game? ... A passion for Christian unity was so often heard to be a passion for an inward looking, comfortable Church. This came home to me at a meeting of the Faith and Order Commission of the World Council of Churches in Lima, Peru. The Commission had just completed the document, *Baptism, Eucharist and Ministry*, perhaps the most important ecumenical document of the ecumenical century, a document that had taken more than 50 years to reach this stage of maturity. As we stood in silent prayer, I looked out of the window. We were staying in a beautiful Roman Catholic retreat centre, an oasis with a stream running through it, with overhanging trees and plants. I noticed that we were fenced in by a high barbed wire fence, and outside our oasis barren steep hills went up. Where the scrub gave way to total barrenness were a few half-built shacks and cardboard boxes where the poor of Lima eked out, God knows how, some sort of living. If what we were doing in our comfortable oasis safeguarding our life-giving traditions of sacraments and ministry had nothing to do with that life then we ought to pack up the doctrinal conversations, which suddenly seemed to me such luxury in that particular context. 'The unity of the Church and the unity of human community, the unity of creation belong inextricably together.' That's a quote from David [Sheppard] and Derek [Worlock]. (Tanner 2013)

> The word 'ecumenical' certainly means 'universal', and the ecumenical movement in its fullest range is a movement for the unity of the Church, covering the whole world. But, without forgetting the universal note, the word ecumenical denotes also (in Archbishop Söderblom's words) 'that spiritual attitude which reflects a deep consciousness of the fundamental oneness of the Christian Church as a whole'. It is the reawakening or creating of that spiritual attitude and finding ways of expressing that fundamental oneness that is the real problem that has to be faced. It is in this deep consciousness of oneness on the part of Christian people, and in a continuing 'spiritual traffic' between the Churches, that the heart of the matter is found.
>
> G. K. A. Bell 1954, p. 162

## The challenge of change

Today, however, further factors have come to the fore relating both to the current position of the churches and to the wider social context. First, all the main denominations are in decline, some in quite steep decline. Paradoxically, there is a sense in which they then become more navel-gazing and retreat into their own institutional interests. This is especially ironic because facing common problems, such as closing local churches, arguably should instead be seen as an opportunity to collaborate more rather than less. Pressures on finance and staffing resources present practical obstacles: fewer clergy, reliance on ageing congregations and the need to maintain costly buildings that are frequently ill-designed or in the wrong place for twenty-first-century ministry. This affects denominations as a whole but also local churches, where the risk is that congregations become more inward-looking and anxious to retain their autonomy in their concern for self-preservation. Significantly, too, the squeeze on budgets tends to affect particularly those areas of ministry that have traditionally focused on social outreach and action, which in turn affects the potential scope for working together in spheres such as justice and peace, social responsibility, industrial and retail chaplaincy.

Mary Tanner underlined this defensiveness and the dangers of churches turning in on themselves in this way:

> Some of our churches having retreated back into their narrow identities and seeming to have no vision of moving into a richer, more diverse, more catholic community, they build higher and higher walls to protect themselves and give up on the sharing that we had so recently established. When funds are tight, ecumenical partnerships and ecumenical staff posts are often the first to be cut. [As a result] our churches are heard by those outside, not least of all by the young, as anti-gay, anti-women, self-absorbed, and when they are interested in Christian unity, they are heard to speak of unity as a kind of 'ecumenical joinery', not of a togetherness where the personal and relational is always prior to the structural and institutional. (Tanner 2013)

## Sharing a rich diversity

Second, 'representative' ecumenism – 'we must have one of you, one of you and one of you' – has always been hard work. It did not necessarily bring together the right people for the task in hand and tended to put a brake on activity. Nowadays, in any case, it is less feasible because the Christian community is much more diverse. The range of Christian churches has widened enormously in our urban areas and presents a much more multifarious pattern of forms of organization and leadership that fits less well with the traditional representative model of working together. This is especially apparent in the larger centres of population, as Colin Marsh, the Ecumenical Development Officer for Birmingham explains:

> If you look at the list of Churches engaged in 1951 who are still predominantly the members of BCT, eight or nine historic Churches would have represented the vast majority of Christians in the city then, and they were organized so you had a Free Churches President, the Catholic Archbishop and the Anglican bishop. So you've got a framework, where together three people can be representative of the Christian community and be seen as such. But there comes a critical point, once you get into the 1990s, and certainly by the 2000s, when that system just doesn't work. And the ecclesiology of the Pentecostal Church traditions and the black-led churches is that each church is much more individual and they don't have a network, which throws up automatically a senior leaders like a bishop or an archbishop or an identifiable network like the Free Churches have. That absence means that I don't think we could try and have a system of organization because it is beyond anyone to do it. The size and scale of black Pentecostal churches across the city means that even the most identifiable leaders can only speak for a small part of that community. (Colin Marsh, interview)

Mary Tanner echoes this observation in relation to the London context:

> Today the players are different. Christian witness is not only given by Anglicans, Roman Catholics and the Free Churches. We live in a different Christian landscape where the fastest growing churches are the Community churches and the Evangelical churches. They are often the ones who run the food banks, the street pastors and work on trafficking.

Then there are the churches established by immigrant communities. Walk from Peckham into town and it's not charity shops that fill the failed local shops but new churches and Christian communities with a variety of unfamiliar names. (Tanner 2013)

> *I think we have all of us moved well beyond ecumenism that wanted unity in everything to a much more grown-up ecumenism, where we recognize that we have different histories and different cultures in different churches, but there is still a great deal where it comes naturally to do it together.*
>
> Malcolm Brown, interview

David Cornick of CTE recognizes that this new landscape is exciting and disturbing in equal measure:

> The world church has arrived on our High Streets, and whilst that is enriching, for it reminds us that Christ transcends culture, it is also uncomfortable because just as Christ transcends cultures, incarnation means that God treasures and inhabits cultures. That's all very well when the cultures are separated by oceans and encounter each other only occasionally in special gatherings like the WCC Assembly, but it's rather more testing when they are on the same street Sunday by Sunday. (Cornick 2013, p. 2)

It all makes for what Bob Fyfe of CTBI refers to as 'liquid ecumenism' on a par with 'liquid modernity', which denotes the shift from a 'heavy' and 'solid', hardware-focused modernity to a 'light' and 'liquid', software-based modernity (Bauman 2000).

The model of a para-church replicating denominational structures, therefore, is no longer appropriate, so that in ecumenical relationships nationally a partnership model of churches retaining and strengthening their integrity in decision-making has replaced the structural model of representative unity. The thrust has become one of co-ordinating the life and work of the churches through networking and partnership to enable the rich diversity of tradition and practice to be shared.

> *Over the next decade, the continuing creation of mutual respect and appreciation has to be at the heart of our work. Relationships have always been vital in ecumenism. They are even more important in this increasingly diverse context. In a sense it is going back to the start of the ecumenical primer. The first leg of CTE's strategy is therefore relationships. Cardinal Cormac Murphy-O'Connor put it superbly when he said 'affective ecumenism is effective ecumenism'.*
> David Cornick 2013

## A relational model of realized unity

At local level, the emphasis now is on encouraging and supporting 'bottom-up' ecumenical activity: 'doing things ecumenically' rather than 'doing ecumenical things'. In other words, more attention is given to joint mission rather than to maintaining what Mary Tanner called the 'ecumenical joinery'. Colin Marsh sees this as positive and, as a Church of England minister in the Liverpool Diocese in the 1980s who remembers the partnerships of those days, he can relate it to his early experience:

Looking at what's going on in terms of Christian unity – the traditional understanding of unity in the last century through the ecumenical movement was unity was a goal to be reached ... What that misses is that alongside that you have another approach to the theology of unity, which is more of a realized unity. So in your common calling to Christ in the community as you live out your faith and as you're doing something and you work alongside somebody of another Christian Church tradition, you discover a unity that is practical and present in the here and now. It is a more realized unity. In some ways you could say that Derek Worlock and David Sheppard and their willingness to work together along with the Free Churches was actually a realized unity. (Colin Marsh, interview)

In some instances this organizational change has also affected the nature of leadership:

What's happening is that the focus is more on relationships. For example, is there somebody from the Christian community who has a relationship with the City Council and is engaging at that level? The Bishop of Birmingham has a fairly strong engagement with the social inclusion process at the moment and I know he is seen by Christians of other traditions as a trusted colleague. Not as their leader but as someone whom they will respect and look up to and will trust his engagement. It is a much more relational model, and that is what we are working to … and I guess when you go back to David Sheppard and Derek Worlock again that is what they were doing. They were mirroring that. (Colin Marsh, interview)

Nor is leadership confined to church leaders. Helped by the rise of social media, a degree of democratization has taken place.

People now tend to work from a very local level through to national or global issues in a much more direct way, and the web and social media are changing all of that beyond recognition. Where previously church leaders and others would take an initiative, and it would come down to a local level for people to become involved in, much more today it's about local people seeing an issue that they're getting through the net, through social media, through news outlets and engaging with that from a local level, back up to national and international engagement. It's not top down, it's bottom up. (Bob Fyfe, CTBI, interview)

## Wider trends

The national and local demographic context is changing in other ways. Society is more plural nowadays in ethnic, cultural and religious terms. The world's other religions have arrived on our doorstep. But also all people of faith face a more secular context, in which it is more difficult to 'keep the rumour of God alive'. For example, in relation to Christianity, fewer people identify themselves as Christian. There is a high degree of

> *The big factor of course is that we, all of us, are in a much more delicate relationship with secular culture. We are in a world that is very impatient with religion in all of its forms and utterly impatient with religious division. We just don't have that luxury anymore.*
>
> Malcolm Brown, interview

religious illiteracy – many children and adults have grown up without any biblical grounding. Although there is evidence of a persistent, widespread deep-seated interest in spirituality, this is often detached from any faith narrative. One response is for churches to seek new and more imaginative ways of reaching out to their communities – mission action plans, fresh expressions, new forms of evangelization. But this increasingly diverse social context has also led to a greater focus on interfaith dialogue and relationships. Sometimes this is primarily to gain a better understanding of other faiths; sometimes it is with a view to developing a multifaith position on external events. In either case, these encounters bring the possibility of deeper conversations, developing mutual trust, building closer relationships and recognizing the scope for joint action.

## Levels of ecumenism

> There is a philosophy for doing ecumenism. Essential to
> this process of unity are relationship and trust, from which
> come reconciliation and unity ... It is a process that occurs
> at all levels of relationship and interaction – including the
> local. Indeed, without the local there would be no basis, no
> foundation for ecumenical endeavour through theologians
> and senior church representatives. There is a symbiotic
> relationship between local and global ecumenism which
> means that each feeds the other, each can inspire the other,
> and neither can make complete progress without the other.
> (Barrett 2012)

Subsidiarity applies to levels of decision-making and activity within
the churches as elsewhere in our society. At the neighbourhood
level, there can be many varieties of organizational arrangements
or expressions of mutual commitment, from local covenants
to Churches Together groups to Single Congregation Local
Ecumenical Partnerships. These can be the springboard not only
to joint prayer and study but also to outreach to, and social action
in, their shared communities. Chapter 5 talks more about such
initiatives: 'The local matters precisely because, in microcosm yet
in reality, the Body of Christ is in that place, in all its fractured
wholeness' (Barrett 2012).

Similarly across wider geographic areas, there are inter-
mediate bodies, such as Churches Together in the Merseyside
Region or West Yorkshire Ecumenical Council (WYEC), that can
encourage, facilitate and support local partnerships and activities
as well as provide forums for the collaboration of church leaders
and arenas for supporting church-related organizations that
operate at regional level, such as ecumenical chaplaincies, and for
links with local authorities and other public bodies.

# ECUMENICAL RELATIONS

## HOW TO GET ON WITH THE CHURCH DOWN THE ROAD

INVITE THEM TO A 'BRING AND SHARE' LUNCH

INVITE THEM TO A PRAYER MEETING

TELEPHONE THE MINISTER, TELLING HIM THAT IF HIS CHURCH EVEN THINKS ABOUT STEALING ANY OF THE YOUNG PEOPLE FROM OUR YOUTH GROUP YOU WILL BE ROUND THERE SO FAST THAT HE WILL NOT EVEN KNOW WHAT HAS HIT HIM

@davewalker

Helen Boothroyd, the Churches Together in Cumbria Social Responsibility Development Officer, describes how this has been very purposefully fostered in Cumbria:

> My role is as a hub for information and networking for what happens at the county and local level ... Ecumenically that is unusual in England. It happens informally elsewhere, but what is unusual in the Cumbrian model is the intentionality of how we have done that for now the best part of nearly 15 years. It's the deliberate giving of time ecumenically to social responsibility and public issues and making sure that it is something the churches are doing together, not just where it happens ad hoc at a local level but intentionally at

the broader county and regional level as well. That ensures full engagement across the denominational spectrum, particularly with partners in the public and third sector ... So in Cumbria for example, if one of the public bodies wants to talk to the faith community, in a lot of places they'll go to the Bishop or the C of E because that's the only visible presence they'll think of for the faith community. In Cumbria, more often now they'll come to Churches Together in Cumbria, because over many years they know us as the faith voice in Cumbria. (Helen Boothroyd, interview)

As at every level of collaboration, the Churches Together bodies for the four nations provide a visible sign of the churches' commitment to deepen their communion with Christ and with one another, and proclaim the gospel together by common witness and service. The headings in the CTE 2014 annual report give an indication of the range of work: supporting Inter-mediate Ecumenism, Pentecostal and Multi-Cultural Relations, Interfaith, Evangelization and Mission.

> *C Scale of ecumenical relationships:*
> *From Conflict*
> *to Competition*
> *to Co-existence*
> *to Co-operation*
> *to Commitment*
> *to Communion*
> *'Experience indicates that the movement is backwards as well as forwards.'*
> Methodist Church, undated

CTBI similarly maintains links across all these areas of work across the four nations. The CTBI website provides a range of resources and news about how Christians are speaking out on and active in relation to a range of peace and conflict issues, such as the arms trade and peace and reconciliation, and social issues, such as asylum seekers and refugees, child protection, criminal justice, economics and poverty, environment, equality, racial justice, social justice and trafficking.

It is perhaps at this level too that the onus particularly lies for doing the necessary theological groundwork for ecumenical activity. The Mission Theology Advisory Group, which is a partnership between CTBI and the Church of England Mission and Public Affairs Division, looks at spirituality, theology, reconciliation, evangelism and mission in our society today. The group's membership reflects its ecumenical nature and brings people together from the four nations.

One example of its work is the Dispossession Project, which provides a set of resources to help us understand more deeply the relationship between God's mission to which we are called and our own social responsibilities to others and to the whole of creation. In the first two years, resources have addressed issues around home and homelessness; care for God's creation; human injustice, limitation of freedom and liberty, including limitation of religious freedom and expression.

## Receptive ecumenism

A term that has come into use over the past few years is 'receptive ecumenism'. In the UK this idea is particularly being developed at the Centre for Catholic Studies at Durham University.

> The essential principle behind Receptive Ecumenism is that the primary ecumenical responsibility is to ask not 'What do the other traditions first need to learn from us?' but 'What do we need to learn from them?' The assumption is that if all were asking this question seriously and acting upon it then all would be moving in ways that would both deepen our authentic respective identities and draw us into more intimate relationship. (Centre for Catholic Studies, undated)

In 2014 the Archbishop of Canterbury, Justin Welby, sent a

message to the ecumenically sponsored Third International Receptive Ecumenism Conference in the USA: 'Ecumenism has a significant place in all that we do. It is the oxygen of Mission and Evangelism and not an extra.' It is also, he said, core to resolving the central problem of the 'broken sign-value we give to the world on account of our state of structural and sacramental fracturing'. He underlined the inseparability of the faith and order and life and work dimensions of ecumenism:

> We are very strong on doing social mission together – and there are some quite remarkable opportunities opening up in this regard at present – but we also need urgently now to complement that with a fresh means of growing together ecclesiastically, organizationally, and theologically. Receptive Ecumenism provides an additional way to take us forward. (Welby 2014)

In other words, he is echoing Ronald Preston's comment quoted near the start of this chapter that the wholeness of the Church must embrace unity and renewal.

## Missio Dei

Mary Tanner's story of Lima illustrates the way 'unity' can too easily be seen as a distraction from the more important task of mission. But the link between mission and unity is a two-way street. Our understanding of mission has changed from the days when it referred primarily to mission fields far away. It has become more all-encompassing:

> We've replaced the old model of mission being something that the church does by the model that mission is of God's essence, that mission is primarily God's mission in Jesus Christ, a reaching out from the heart of the Trinity to bring forth and redeem creation. Mission then becomes in Rowan

Williams's words, 'finding out where the Holy Spirit is and joining in'. The shorthand term is *Missio Dei* (mission of God). If that understanding is right, mission becomes a springboard for unity. (Cornick 2013, p. 3)

> This theology is founded in the essential unity of the three persons of the godhead: Father, Son and Holy Spirit. The church is called to participate in the working of God who, through the sending of the Son, is actively seeking to reconcile the whole of creation. Consequently, knowingly or unknowingly, as churches participate in God's mission they are all participating in the same mission. Since God is one, united in the Trinity, Missio Dei challenges churches to become reconciled with each other in order to participate together in a mission in which Christians and churches are assumed to be equal partners. This mission theology is for all who are committed to Christian unity.
>
> Colin Marsh and Jim Currin 2013, p. 4

*Missio Dei* 'places Christian mission at the heart of the life of the churches – all Christians, whether lay or clergy, are called to participate as co-partners with Christ. Christian unity is to be expressed by churches of different traditions sharing in mission' (Marsh and Currin 2013, p. 7).

# 4
# A Church Shaped by the Periphery

*'The Church [is[ not an NGO but a love story.' 'The ideal of a missionary, poor Church.' 'A Church shaped by the periphery.' 'We are among the wounds of Jesus. These wounds need to be recognized, and listened to.'*

Ivereigh 2014, pp. 86, 87, quoting Pope Francis

*Solving the world's problems requires a commitment to a very ancient idea whose time has urgently come: the common good. How do we work together, even with people we don't agree with? How do we treat each other, especially the poorest and most vulnerable? How do we take care not just of ourselves but also one another? How do we move beyond interests of left and right and become accountable to a higher good? Only by inspiring a spiritual and practical commitment to the common good can we make our personal and public lives better.*

Jim Wallis 2013, p. xi

How we live, what we do and how we do it will naturally and rightly vary. In Chapters 5 and 6, I shall give examples of the many dimensions of the Church being active in society. But first it may be useful to try to get a handle on this diversity by looking at different *levels* of involvement and different *types* of involvement in the world.

## Levels of involvement

There are many levels of involvement: individual, local church, Christian group or organization, church leadership, institutional activity by churches, such as running schools and providing social care. In all of these spheres, what we are and what we do is as important – or even more important – than what we say.

*The way we are* applies to us as individuals. We see from Jesus' ministry that people were moved and convicted as much by his bearing and the implicit messages conveyed as by the way he behaved. This was what swayed the centurion witnessing his death. The totality of our lives will be more expressive than anything we say: not just whether we go to church or give to charity or are kind to the lady next door, but our lifestyle more broadly: where we live if we have a choice, send our children to school or shop; how we support our local community, how willingly we pay our taxes and how we decide how to vote.

> *The* live*simply project, launched in 2006, was inspired by Pope Paul VI's encyclical Populorum Progressio.* live*simply's key message is: 'God calls us to look hard at our lifestyles and to choose to live simply, sustainably and in solidarity with the poor. In this way we can help create a world in which human dignity is respected and everyone can reach their full potential. This would be true progress, worth more than economic growth alone.'*
>
> live*simply, undated*

*The way we are* applies to the local mission and ministry of the Church. Over 20 years ago Don May and Margaret Simey contributed to a series of occasional papers on Church and society. Don May was the minister at Princes Park Methodist Church in Granby, Liverpool 8 through the 1960s. Margaret Simey lived in the area and was a councillor for the Granby Ward. Their paper 'The Servant Church in Granby' was an account of how an inner-city church found itself forced by sheer weight of circumstance to move from the 'gathered church' model of ministry, focusing largely on its own membership, to one that

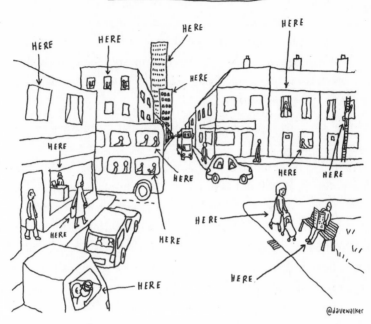

acknowledged the importance of accountability for and to the community it was there to serve. It was a story of ecumenism before the better-known story of ecumenism in Liverpool! One of the most interesting dimensions of the story was Margaret Simey's observation – from the perspective of a sympathetic fellow traveller rather than a believer – of the real value of the Church's role and presence (some of which I have already quoted):

> In effect, the churches stood for an alternative way of life to that of the individualism and materialism which threatened our survival as a human society. Their efforts were often as futile as our own but I am convinced that merely to exist amongst us on those terms was a positive contribution ... the struggle to keep alive any sense of social duty is often a desperate one. The mere existence in our midst of a handful

43

of people who were there for no other reason than to keep that flag flying I believe to have been of greater importance than we, or perhaps they realized. There was unspoken comfort to be derived from the fact that someone still had faith in the ideal of the caring community even though bitter disillusion had eroded our own conviction. (Don May and Margaret Simey 1989)

In this story the apparently paradoxical nature of the Church's ministry emerges. Total involvement in the real arena of people's lives had to be combined with standing for a deeper reality than the political, social and economic. The Church represented an element of stability, an enduring faithful presence in Granby, so that the flux and uncertainty all around could be more bravely confronted. Hopelessness waited round every corner because of the scale of human need; the Church shared the anguish but also embodied a future hope.

Tim Bissett, recalling his experience as chief executive of the Church Urban Fund, also emphasizes the importance of 'sticking around'.

Most faith-based projects are able to undertake things with a much longer-term perspective ... If you look at many deprived communities, the only real service delivery that is left, or the only organizations that tend to be left, are housing associations and churches. In the current context most other organizations have just withdrawn, and so where you have a faith context and a group of people who live and are participant in that community they tend to stick around for much longer and are therefore more effective. (Tim Bissett, interview)

A current example from Liverpool is St Andrew's Church, Clubmoor. The vicar, Steve McGanity, talks about their approach:

My being here for 16 years has helped ... It has helped us to pursue a particular direction over a long period of time. So we have a separate charitable company that does all of our community action work. That has been set up for ten years ... we started small with one pilot project, and it has grown, and as things have grown people have become more involved in it. It has changed the nature of the church congregation as well. The church congregation is now younger. Around 40 per cent of the congregation have addiction problems (we do an annual survey of the congregation) ... or diagnosed mental health issues ... So the congregation has changed during that time, which has enabled us to keep the whole process of engaging with the local community and to increase that engagement ... We've had people move to the area who were already church members, but saw what we were trying to do, and moved from 'better' areas in terms of their social make-up, to be in the area and to be part of the whole process of engaging with the local community. We've had about four families doing that. (Steve McGanity, interview)

*The way we are* applies to groups and organizations. Church Action on Poverty (CAP) is a national ecumenical Christian social justice charity, committed to tackling poverty in the UK. CAP works in partnership with churches and with people in poverty themselves to find solutions to poverty, locally, nationally and globally. Founded in the mid 1980s, it tried to move from speaking for and acting on behalf of those in poverty to working in partnership with them. All those involved were changed as a result. It was not only right; it was more effective. Once it put a priority on including those usually excluded from the policy debate, CAP was certainly more convincing and arguably more influential. As Niall Cooper, the present Director of CAP, says:

Do we treat people in poverty as an undeserving underclass, hapless victims, or potential agents for change and transformation? As we are discovering in our work at Church Action on Poverty, ordinary people can do extraordinary things. Contrary to the growing view that people on low incomes are dysfunctional, dependent shirkers and skivers, Church Action on Poverty's experience has proved again and again that people in poverty not only understand the root causes of their problems, but are highly effective at creating lasting solutions to them. Over the last 30 plus years, Church Action on Poverty has worked alongside thousands of people from some of the poorest, most neglected communities across the UK, supporting, educating and empowering individuals to effect change from within. Instead of imposing policies or top-down solutions, we use radical, participatory tools that help people in poverty access power and education, creating a network of grassroots social change that continues to grow. (Niall Cooper, interview)

Listening and being involved on the ground is stressed by Annie Merry of Faiths4Change, an environmental initiative that works across North West England:

Listening is very important, partly to the beneficiaries, and also getting out there. There's no substitute to walking the beat, so to speak, and actually getting out there and meeting with people and listening to what else is going on in their area. It's not just what you can bring, it's what is already happening, and then maybe drawing up something on the basis of what's missing ... or sometimes it can mean going back another day, because you're actually not needed. (Annie Merry, interview)

Whatever the virtues of faith-based groups, it is important to guard against any claim that they are necessarily inherently morally superior. Many secular bodies share their qualities and principles. This is partly because they are not exclusive to Christians, but also because individuals of faith have often been the moving spirit behind setting up and shaping these other groups.

*The way we are* applies to the churches nationally. As major institutions, how far are they modelling the sorts of community they advocate to others? Employment and pay policies have been in the news recently in relation to zero-hours contracts and the living wage. Claire Dove is a Roman Catholic who is chief

> [N]ine tenths of the work of the Church in the world is done by Christian people fulfilling responsibilities and performing tasks which in themselves are not part of the official system of the Church at all.
> William Temple 1942, p. 18

executive of Blackburne House Women's Technology Centre in Liverpool, chair of the Liverpool Fairness Commission and chair of Social Enterprise UK. She asks some challenging questions:

> Churches need to start making changes closer to home ... They are still powerful institutions, but how are they using that power? They are big employers, but what are they doing to promote equal opportunities? They are social enterprises too, but where is their sense of enterprise; what are their procurement policies doing for the local community, what are they asking of their suppliers, and where is the added value of their investments? (T4CG conference 2013)

In his book *Belonging*, Peter Selby talks about faith combining delight in God's creation with the perception of the universe as fallen and a consequent longing for it to come to its intended wholeness. God delights in what God has made and God longs for the world to be as God intends. Delight and longing are at the heart of life's meaning and direction whether we recognize it or not. Selby talks about the Church as 'the first fruit of God's

47

longing, the instrument by which that longing is expressed in its prayer and its action' (1991, p. 2). His book is concerned about the kind of community the Church is called to be which, if it is to express the longing of God, has to be a very different way of being a community. But it is also about how 'the Church is in great danger of forgetting that essential point about the manner of its existence in the world'. All human communities draw lines around themselves. They define insiders at the expense of outsiders. The Church is a human community, but it is also the first fruit of God's longing.

> *In any setting the ability of the church to minister to the nation depends on the seriousness with which it seeks to exemplify in its own life the message it proclaims.*
>
> Duncan Forrester 1989, p. 64

> Its life together, therefore, does not depend on excluding people and groups, but on a witness to the constantly inclusive activity of God whose concern extends even to a sparrow that falls to the ground. When that is forgotten, as inevitably and frequently it is, the Church becomes absorbed in various kinds of defence mechanism. In the process of exclusion in which it then engages, the Church ends up removing from itself the very sources of grace and hope from which it draws its life. (Selby 1991, p. 3)

Selby is talking about the Church of England. No doubt others can see contradictions in their own churches between the gospel they preach and the message conveyed by their structures, organization and institutional behaviour.

## Types of involvement

Another way of considering the Church in the world is to look at different types of involvement that are not necessarily mutually exclusive or always easy to disentangle in real life:

- *Pastoral activity/provision of care*: Within the home or among neighbours, or in an organized way within Christian or secular organizations.

- *Prayer*: This is a very active interaction with and ministry to the world. Yet prayer and action often seem to be counterpoised rather than juxtaposed. Contemplation is seen as an alternative rather than a forerunner to action. How often do we see – and are we encouraged to see – worship more generally as a retreat from the world rather than an equipping for it? Perhaps even worse is the implication that Church is where we find God: a very partial view and one that potentially distorts our discipleship.

- *Partnership*: There are often opportunities to join in service with allies – other Christians and people of other faiths or none – and benefits to be gained. However, sometimes this will present dilemmas as other people's agendas – including those of funding bodies – will rarely be a perfect fit with our own, and therefore partnership must be carefully considered in order not to lose sight of our essential values.

- *Public theology*: This can often supply concepts and a vocabulary that are relevant to/resonate with people's concerns even when they have no Christian attachment. The goals of public policy, such as 'healthy communities', 'well-being', 'resilience' and 'sustainability', are all ones on which we ought to have something both distinctive and recognizably relevant to say.

- *Political involvement*: Much of the framework for our social and economic relationships is set in place through political mechanisms at local, national or international levels, and therefore there is a need for a Christian voice and presence at all these levels.

- *Prophecy*: This is the essential task of trying to identify the signs of the times – see where we are deviating from God's plan for his world; and trying to anticipate key issues rather than jumping belatedly onto already departing bandwagons.

## Contribution to civil society

In 2003 there was a survey of more than 2,300 faith groups in the North West across eight faiths to examine the contribution of faith communities to civil society in the region; that is, going beyond worship activities. The report of the survey, *Faith in England's Northwest*, showed:

- the breadth of faith community groups' involvement in projects to address homelessness, racism, crime, drug and alcohol abuse, skills development, and environmental projects;
- extensive involvement in providing services for older people and children and within more deprived communities;
- that faith communities are strongest where there is greatest social need, and in areas with few community facilities, faith buildings can provide an important local amenity;
- that faith communities bring visitors and provide a welcome for visitors – think of the cathedrals and the role they play, not only in attracting tourists but also as a quiet space for individuals and a shared space for the many for major events either for celebration or collective sorrow;
- that faith communities are significant patrons of sports and cultural activities, such as choral and instrumental music, dance, drama and the visual arts;
- that faith communities play a strong supportive role, often in times of crisis – for example, 45 per cent of rural churches responding to the survey indicated they had participated in support initiatives during the foot and mouth crisis in 2001;
- that faith communities stimulate a huge amount of

volunteering – a later example was the floods in Carlisle in 2005, when the churches mobilized 400 volunteers within a couple of days, who continued to offer hospitality and to help out for many months after the immediate problem had disappeared from the headlines;

- that the stickability of faith communities is often significant – just by being there, they are serving a purpose, providing a 'faithful presence';
- that representatives of faith communities are often active in partnerships, such as in regeneration schemes, and can be valuable partners because of their intimate *lived* knowledge of the area and because they frequently have access to those people others find hard to reach;
- that multifaith bodies enable faith communities to 'speak to the powers' collectively from a shared value base.

The survey was valuable in a number of ways. First, it enabled some of the faith communities' contributions to be quantified: to say X per cent do this and X per cent do that. Measurability is not the whole story and some things that are equally or more valuable are impossible to quantify. Nevertheless it is very useful when talking to public agencies, especially if organizations are seeking funding. Second, the survey was a revelation to faith communities themselves because it put what they were doing in a wider social and economic context. Though they very often thought they were just doing 'what comes naturally', it showed that, in fact, they were also contributing to small 'p' political goals such as regeneration, social inclusion or sustainable development. Cutting through the jargon on both sides, it showed there are shared goals that faith communities are already pursuing whether or not they have previously articulated it in quite this way. It gave them a new confidence and a new vocabulary for conversations with local authorities or other public agencies.

## Forms of social capital

A follow-up study to *Faith in England's Northwest* focused on 12 faith-based projects and sought to evaluate their contribution to social and economic well-being. It found that faith-based organizations can stand to be judged alongside other voluntary bodies in terms of the credibility and quality of their service provision and that some are uniquely positioned to deliver projects tackling social cohesion issues. Inevitably they face the same organizational challenges: capacity, resources, governance and management of volunteers. But because many are rooted in their local communities, they provide a level of continuity and sustained support that it may be hard for others to match. This can create a virtuous circle generating local trust, commitment and financial or in-kind resources.

A term that has become current over the last decade and a half – though its origins are much older – is 'social capital'. In his book *Bowling Alone* in 2000, the American author Robert Putnam argued that while Americans had become much wealthier, their sense of community had withered. Neighbourhoods had become more anonymous. They suffered from a decline in community networks and this represented a loss of social capital. It is disputable whether social ties are eroding or simply evolving and it is arguable that the term 'social capital' is too vague and hard to measure to be useful. Even the use of the word 'capital' is off-putting to some people because it seems to reduce everything to currency. However, the concept can be a helpful counterbalance to the idea of financial or physical capital – an acknowledgement of the value of human capital and the need to invest in strengthening social relationships and networks. The increasing importance given to the idea of social capital derives from recognition that the *quality* of our relationships matters not only to our individual lives but also to our common life – the ties that bind, the glue that holds communities together. And it is an idea that has added significance in a time of fast-moving change, in a society with extremes of poverty and wealth and in communities that are increasingly diverse.

There are different types of social capital. The first is *bonding*, which refers to close connections between people, their networks of families and friends and the bonds within communities. These can of course be supportive and enriching, but they can be excluding to outsiders. Even for insiders they may be constraining. A study in a former East Midlands mining village found that relations in some parts of the community were very strong indeed – people relied on them and there was a robust community spirit. However, there were some deep divisions in the community as well: historic divides that saw groups and families falling out, sometimes for decades – some, for example, were still fighting the miners' strike of the mid 1980s. In addition there was a danger of entrenching a sort of siege mentality that isolated residents from wider society. Conversely the area was stereotyped in the outside world: seen as 'no-go', with the danger of being shunned by agencies and employers (Bennett et al. 2000).

Within faith-based groups too there is always a danger of a silo mentality – a wish to stay within the comfort zone of like-minded people – that is a barrier to collaboration. So although bonding is important, it needs to be accompanied by broader outlets and horizons or *bridging* social capital; that is, the weaker but more cross-cutting ties that span people with less in common. It may be different geographic communities or different communities of interest – ethnic, cultural or faith groups or different generations. Citizens UK is an example of an organization in which churches, schools, mosques, trade unions and other civil society organizations work together for the common good. As an alliance, Citizens UK also promotes the third type of social capital, *linking*, which means formal and informal ties between a community and decision-makers or service providers, cutting across both similarity and status, and enabling people to exert influence and reach resources outside their usual circles.

The three types are interdependent. *Bonding* social capital is an essential foundation for building the confidence, trust and capacity to engage both with other communities and with decision-makers. *Bridging* can begin to allow different groups to share different perspectives, overcome prejudices and address joint problems and work towards solutions that respect difference but work for everyone. *Linking* social capital gives communities the means of influencing decisions affecting their area or interests.

> *From a governmental point of view, the social capital and, specifically, the faithful capital offered by Christian churches and other faith organisations can be seen as both a valuable resource and as a source of discomfiture. Commitment to neighbourhood, long-term presence, strong value base, important community facilities, bridging inter-faith networks – they all offer paths to the grails of 'community cohesion' and 'urban regeneration'. On the other hand, the distinct and conflicting language of faith, the values that challenge rather than support government policy, and working styles that fail to mesh with time-limited, benchmark-driven outcome-required government schemes, all pose a challenge.*
>
> *Faithful Cities* 2006, p. 3

Putnam identified faith groups as having a significant contribution to make to social capital because of their shared values and because they are socially rooted. At best it is a concept that resonates strongly with theological precepts such as human worth and dignity, hospitality, love for neighbour and care for the stranger. The idea has been developed further to try to pinpoint what faith groups might particularly bring, although a similar cautionary note should be sounded with a reminder that, as with social capital, 'faithful capital' is not necessarily wholly benign. For some groups within churches and other faith communities, being tightly bonded and deriving mutual support brings an unhealthy 'us against the world' stance rather than giving the security and confidence that allows openness to others.

In the UK it is the William Temple Foundation that has led the way in researching and articulating the contribution of faith groups in civil renewal. Two terms are used. 'Religious capital' denotes the 'what' and the 'how': the practical contribution that faith groups make to society by creating networks of trust and support through their activities and use of buildings. 'Spiritual capital' speaks of the 'why': this gives the 'theological identity and worshipping tradition, but also a value system, moral vision and a basis for faith' (Baker and Skinner 2006).

A criticism that can be made of both social capital and faithful capital is that they can ignore the questions of power and fail to acknowledge the conflicting and different interests in society. Parallel debates sometimes recur about social work and community work. Do they only enable people to bear the unbearable, tolerate the intolerable? Do they in that sense collude with the powers and help to prop up inequitable systems? Social capital alone cannot compensate for the lack of other forms of capital so that the questions must always be asked: 'Who exactly are we bonding, bridging and linking with, and for whom?' and 'What issues of control are being created?' (Davey 2007, p. 17)

The next chapter illustrates the variety of ways Christian and other faith groups work together to serve their communities, locally and nationally, and how, at the same time, they address some of these more challenging questions.

# 5
# Who is my Neighbour?

*Social action is not an optional side project for the Church;
it is core to its heart and mission. The commitment to this
calling can be clearly seen in the scale and diversity of activities
offered by local churches ... Not only do churches offer services
that meet specific needs, they also create spaces for people to
connect with and get to know others, helping to build stronger
and more resilient communities.*

Church Urban Fund/Church of England 2015, p. 1

The common good draws its significance directly from the
second great commandment. When asked which is the greatest
commandment in the law, Jesus said:

> 'You shall love the Lord your God with all your heart, and with
> all your soul, and with all your mind.' This is the greatest and
> first commandment. And a second is like it: 'You shall love
> your neighbour as yourself.' On these two commandments
> hang all the law and the prophets. (Matthew 22.36–40)

The follow-up question was 'Who is my neighbour?', which Jesus
answered by telling the parable of the Good Samaritan (Luke
10.29–37). In this story of a man robbed and beaten on the road
from Jerusalem to Jericho, a priest and a Levite both scurry past
without offering help. Surprisingly, it is the Samaritan traveller
who comes to the man's aid – surprising because Samaritans
were looked down on and ostracized, and he might well have felt
justified in ignoring the injured man. But in practice he looked

beyond any prejudices based on race or religion and just saw someone in need, whom he then helped compassionately and practically.

The point is further developed in the story of the sheep and the goats (Matthew 25.31–45), which identifies service to God as inextricable from service to others: 'just as you did it to one of the least of these who are members of my family, you did it to me ... just as you did not do it to one of the least of these, you did not do it to me.' The pursuit of the common good through Christian community action, therefore, is a direct response to both the two commandments at the heart of the Christian faith.

## Public issues and private troubles

The last chapter indicated a little of the breadth of faith communities' contribution to civil society. In the course of this activity they can frequently shine a spotlight on problems that often remain below the radar of public consciousness or that people in power are reluctant to tackle. An abiding feature of the voluntary, community and faith sector is staying connected with people's lives and being aware of social undercurrents not otherwise being confronted. A striking example over the last few years has been engaging with the rise of food poverty. A Church of England survey by the Church Urban Fund (Church Urban Fund/Church of England 2015) showed that comparing church activities in 2011 and 2014, the percentage involved in food banks had risen from 33 per cent to 66 per cent. The nature of foodbank activity spanned:

- collecting food
- providing volunteers
- helping to manage
- giving out vouchers
- offering church premises.

Other food poverty activity included providing food or giving money for food when asked and cooking regular meals for people at risk of food poverty.

There are a number of ways that such activities can be supported nationally.

The **Together Network** is being developed by the Church Urban Fund (CUF). It comprises joint ventures with Church of England dioceses to work with local churches and groups to support them in the work they are already doing and help its extension and enhancement to bring about positive changes in their localities. The aims of the Network are to increase the number of church-based social activities; to develop people's capacity to take effective action to tackle poverty; to build partnerships and collaboration between churches and with other organizations in order to increase joined-up working and innovation. For example, Preston Christian Action Network operates under the umbrella of Together Lancashire in co-ordinating and supporting the work of Christian social activists and community projects linked to the various denominations. Working in a multifaith context, Together Lancashire also collaborates well with the Preston Faith Forum (Greg Smith 2015a).

> As well as encouraging the development of new activities, the Network also aims to build the capacity of churches and local organizations to take effective action to tackle poverty. As such, Development Workers run workshops, courses and events to inform people about poverty-related issues, share best practice responses and enable practitioners to develop new skills. Over the last 18 months, the Network has taken part in more than 415 events, attended by almost 8,000 people. In Cornwall, the Joint Venture has hosted several 'Meet the Funder' events in which over 300 church

leaders and staff of community organizations have met with funders and received training on how to write effective funding applications ... In Liverpool, the Development Worker organized a city-wide conference to raise awareness of the difficulties faced by asylum seekers in the city; in Middlesbrough, the Joint Venture hosted the Bridges of Hope conference that brought together local churches and organizations and raised awareness of the issues faced by local people. Elsewhere, other Joint Ventures have hosted briefing sessions to build understanding and awareness of topics such as welfare reform, food poverty and credit unions. (Church Urban Fund and Charity Evaluation Services 2014)

*A survey conducted by Together Middlesbrough in 2013 sought to quantify the scale and range of social action undertaken by churches and Christian projects across Middlesbrough. This showed that:*

- *98 per cent of responding churches and Christian projects are engaged in at least one activity to address a social need;*
- *together, these churches and projects are running a total of 276 activities amounting to approximately 800 hours of social action each week;*
- *an army of over 1,000 volunteers is involved in organized Christian social action, benefiting over 5,000 people in local communities every week;*
- *churches and Christian projects offer a wide range of social action activities. They are more likely to be working with children and young people, women, the elderly and asylum seekers and least likely to be providing activities that tackle unemployment, homelessness, addictions or offer support to ex-offenders;*
- *many churches are working jointly with other churches and*

> *community groups, but there are fewer partnerships with*
> *local authorities and other statutory agencies;*
> * *Christian social action has grown in the past two years, and*
>   *74 per cent of churches and projects have plans for further*
>   *developments.*
>   Church Urban Fund and the Church of England 2015

The **Near Neighbours Programme** is another national programme run by the Church Urban Fund (CUF). It focuses on multifaith areas across England, currently in the north-west towns of Bury, Rochdale, Oldham and Burnley; Leeds, Bradford and Dewsbury in Yorkshire; in Birmingham, Wolverhampton, Sandwell, Walsall and Dudley, Leicester and Nottingham in the West and East Midlands; and in Luton and across most of London in the south. The purpose is both to help people from different faiths get to know and understand each other better and to encourage people of different faiths and of no faith to come together for initiatives that improve their local neighbourhood. One of the advantages of each of these local initiatives having a national 'parent' is that CUF can also connect them with other national partners such as the Muslim Christian Forum, the Hindu Christian Forum and the Council of Christians and Jews.

**Faith in Community Scotland** (FiCS), which was established in 2005, represents another way of supporting national and local initiatives. Its key aim is to relieve poverty by supporting the faith groups working in the most disadvantaged communities through training, resources, advice and other forms of engagement. FiCS operates as an 'umbrella organization', with a number of different projects existing as part of the wider organization.

* The ***Transformation Team*** provides training, facilitation and support to local faith communities in Glasgow, Lanarkshire and Ayrshire to develop and sustain anti-poverty projects.

- *Faith in Community Dundee* fulfils a similar role to the *Transformation Team* but in Dundee, Scotland's second poorest city.
- *Faith in Throughcare* supports prisoners and their families as they move from prison back into their local communities, and enables faith and community groups to provide specialist support and befriending for people leaving prison.
- *Faiths in Scotland Community Action Fund* (FiSCAF) provides small grants to faith-based groups tackling poverty across Scotland.
- The *Poverty Truth Commission* brings together some of Scotland's most influential leaders and some of the country's poorest citizens to address poverty, aiming to effect policy change by facilitating these relationships between people living in poverty and decision-makers.
- *Tackling Sectarianism Together* works with local churches in the west of Scotland to help them improve relationships across sectarian divides.

The core team works alongside to provide overall strategic leadership together with opportunities for shared learning, reflection and research.

**CSAN – Caritas Social Action Network** – is the agency of the Catholic Bishops' Conference of England and Wales for domestic social action. The family of social action charities and dioceses that work with the most vulnerable people in our society form the Caritas network supported by the CSAN team through, for instance, special-interest forums, peer support and theological reflection. A further advantage of having a national network is that it can have a more powerful voice in advocacy and attempting to exert influence on the policy issues that are critical to their service users.

The **National Justice and Peace Network** of the Roman Catholic Church in England and Wales is currently focusing mainly on poverty and inequality. It addresses issues relating to fairer taxes and social security benefits, the living wage and justice in the workplace. It seeks to raise awareness about environmental justice issues and about ethical investment, working with the Ecumenical Council on Corporate Responsibility. At diocesan level, Justice and Peace Commissions may cover very diverse issues ranging from cancelling the debts of the world's poorest countries to housing and homelessness in England and Wales and support for asylum seekers and refugees.

The **Joint Public Issues Team** of the Baptist Union of Great Britain, the Methodist Church, the United Reformed Church and the Church of Scotland helps the four churches work together on issues of justice and inequality as well as social issues more widely, and produces study and worship resources for individuals and local churches.

In addition to these bodies that are formally linked to the institutional Church, there is now a growing number of national organizations that exercise ministries focusing on specific areas of work. Some operate a franchise model; for example, the Trussell Trust in relation to food banks and Christians Against Poverty who run services such as debt help and job clubs through local churches. Street Pastors are one strand of mission under the umbrella of the interdenominational Ascension Trust, founded by Les Isaac. He started the Street Pastors Initiative in 2003 in response to growing concern about problems such as gun and knife crime, gang culture, binge drinking and the associated fear in communities. Street pastors are trained volunteers from local churches who patrol in teams in city and town centres on Friday and Saturday nights to care for people out on the streets, working in collaboration with police and other agencies. All these specialist ministries can be seen as responses to increasingly evident need. The role of the national bodies is to provide expertise and facilitate and support local projects.

## Creating new and hopeful possibilities

> Participation in projects seeking to *actualize* the common good is one way in which its benefits can be realized by all. If the common good is rooted in 'the local', then it is through experiencing the difference it can make at grassroots that we can begin to embrace it as a mode of politics. From schoolchildren identifying issues of concern in their local neighbourhood and preparing cost-effective and creative solutions for submission to their local authority, to people with divergent perspectives and interests on specific topics coming together to listen, dialogue and generate new and mutually beneficial ideas for action, the common good can prove its value as a new kind of conversation that goes beyond old divisions – left and right, business and unions, secular and faith, local and national – to create new and hopeful possibilities. (Andrew Bradstock, in Sagovsky and McGrail 2015, pp. 27–8; emphasis in original)

A 2012 study for the Church of England on Resourcing Christian Community Action looked at a wide spectrum of examples of Christian community action. It covered policy areas ranging from homelessness to food banks; employment and training to debt counselling; youth projects to care for the elderly; befriending to social enterprise; street pastors to lunch clubs; counselling to advocacy and campaigning. Examples spanned rural, urban and suburban locations and included denominational, ecumenical and interfaith initiatives. Although most were in materially deprived areas, Christian community action is called for in any context to demonstrate both care for neighbours and new ways of being, and to work for personal, social and structural transformation. In the 2015 survey of church-based social action conducted by the Church Urban Fund and the Church of England, isolation or loneliness was the issue most commonly cited as a major or significant problem. Although more common in the most deprived areas, it was nevertheless significant in most of the wealthier areas too.

A wealth of projects and organizations could be used to illustrate their many ways of pursuing the common good, but space does not allow. It would be impossible even to attempt a comprehensive list. In any case, it may be more telling to say a little more about a few.

## Longbenton: re-engaging with the community

The first is an example from one of the CUF joint ventures which shows how the more open and creative use of a church hall can transform the church's relationship with the local community.

The new vicar in Longbenton, North Tyneside, approached Together Newcastle (our Joint Venture with the Diocese of Newcastle) for help in re-engaging the church with its local community. As the area has high levels of poverty and very few meeting places, she wanted to redevelop the run-down church hall in order to make it more accessible for the community. The Development Worker met with the vicar and the congregation several times, helping them to think about their mission in the area and secure funds to refurbish the building. Following its redevelopment, the church hall now hosts several weekly community activities including a youth club, community open day, lunch club and community choir. These activities enable people from the local community to meet and get to know one another, helping to reduce isolation and tackle poverty of relationship. The vicar reflected, 'I really don't know where I would have begun without [the Development Worker] ... he was a guardian angel at the end of a telephone call' (Church Urban Fund and Charity Evaluation Services 2014).

## Hope+ Foodbank

Hope+ Foodbank is a partnership between Liverpool Anglican Cathedral, the Roman Catholic Metropolitan Cathedral of Christ the King, St Bride's Church and other city centre faith communities. People can go hungry for reasons ranging from redundancy to receiving an unexpected bill while on a low income. Partner agencies – Social Services, GPs, CAB and other charities – not only distribute vouchers to those in need of emergency food relief to people experiencing crisis in the inner city area, but also help by providing a network of additional support in areas such as housing, debt and benefit advice, and assistance in finding and preparing for employment. In addition, partnership with the British Red Cross and other related agencies has enabled the provision of emergency support to newly arrived victims of civil unrest in Syria, Iraq and other countries. Often arriving with nothing but the clothes they are wearing, and deeply traumatized, Hope+ is able to offer a warm welcome from its volunteers and practical help with food and clothing.

> To us, the + in HOPE+ is the really important bit. Just handing people a bag of food:
> - can create dependency
> - does not solve any problem other than immediate need
> - does not allow us to be advocates for our guests
> - is not what God asks of us
> - is not why Christ died for us. (Hope+ Foodbank, undated)

## *Places of Welcome*

The Places of Welcome activity was one of the key outcomes of Birmingham city's Social Inclusion Process. It aims to establish places where isolated and vulnerable people – which could be any of us at particular moments – can be welcomed and supported. Thrive Together Birmingham has been instrumental in developing this project. Over the last year, Thrive Together has drawn on its contacts from the faith and voluntary sector to identify potential partners, secure their participation, deliver training sessions for network members and facilitate the development of a Charter of Welcome. There are currently 42 active Places of Welcome across the city and now extending beyond it to Sandwell and Wolverhampton, including several churches, a Gudwara, a residents association and a convent; a further 30 organizations are exploring the possibility of joining the network. Thrive continues to identify new partners and has developed a Places of Welcome website – www.placesofwelcome.org – that will allow people who are new to the city to find out where they can receive a warm welcome. Each place of welcome is committed to the 5 Ps:

1 **Place**: An accessible and hospitable building, open at the same time every week for people to drop in.
2 **People**: Open to everyone regardless of their circumstances or situation, and staffed by volunteers committed to offering generous hospitality and creating an informal and relaxed environment.
3 **Presence**: A place where people actively listen to one another, treating each person as an individual and not seeking to categorize or box them by their needs or disadvantage.
4 **Provision**: Offering free refreshments (at least a cup of tea and a biscuit) and basic information and sign posting information to city-wide organizations. This will be compiled centrally and made available to coordinators of each venue.

5   ***Participation***: Recognizing that every person coming to a Place of Welcome will bring talents, experiences and skills that they might be willing to share locally, and actively encouraging people to use their skills and abilities at the Place of Welcome or in wider community projects and activities.

## L'Arche

L'Arche is a worldwide federation of people with and without learning difficulties working together for a world where all belong.

L'Arche is actually very small and insignificant in terms of the number of people that we directly support. But in our charter, over and over again it talks about being a sign and in a way our contribution to the common good is also about being a sign saying 'in choosing to live with difference; in choosing to live together; we are saying it's possible; it's good; and to be fully human we have to welcome all of ourselves and each other ... It's in living with people and sharing life with people that you discover that I am just as vulnerable and as marginalized and as poor as anybody else is because we are all fundamentally equal.' (John Sargent, L'Arche, interview)

The principles that are important in each L'Arche community are:

- ***Servant leadership***: roles and structures are at the service of the mission. People are called to leadership roles for limited terms after discernment processes. Those in authority gain wisdom through listening and taking counsel.
- ***Partnership***: the structures are to foster a dynamic of trust and collaboration.
- ***Subsidiarity***: matters are dealt at the most appropriate level closest to the people affected, and only when they cannot be solved there are they referred to another level.
- ***Accountability*** is about being responsible and being linked

to the wider body. It is also about taking responsibility for the consequences of one's actions.

- **Participation**: effective communication is essential. Processes are defined, published and open. They include people with and without a learning disability.
- **Inculturation**: L'Arche Communities live in different cultures. L'Arche embraces this diversity while engaging in an ongoing process of reciprocal and critical interaction, adaptation and challenge.
- **Solidarity**: all in L'Arche share a common humanity and a fundamental equality. We have a shared responsibility for each other and are committed to the common good.

---

Seed to Soup, L'Arche Liverpool

*This project promotes wellbeing and healthy eating among people with and without learning disabilities. By using an existing sensory garden and building new raised beds, it safeguarded a green space, increased physical activity for individuals as they learnt new skills and connected with other participants and volunteers. There are now social worker referrals to the project (social prescribing) and 'we have been able to network with other organisations to our great benefit'.*

A case study in Natural Choices for Health and Wellbeing
Evaluation Report 2015 www.merseyforest.org.uk

---

## Parish Power

Parish Power is a project of the Justice and Peace Commission in Liverpool Roman Catholic Archdiocese and supported financially by the Passionists, because it fits with issues they addressed for many years in Liverpool 8. It was set up to explore how to help parishes develop an energy policy that saves money by cutting energy use and helps parishioners to do the same by training volunteers to signpost people to expert advice. The prompt for the project was Kevin, a senior manager in a construction firm, being made redundant. The idea crystallized when he attended a class on Catholic Social Teaching while he was thinking how he could continue to deploy his skills. A small team took it forward, including the Archdiocesan Justice and Peace fieldworker and a Faiths4Change worker. CUF gave funding thanks to assistance from another long-standing partner, the Anglican Diocese of Liverpool's Department of Church and Society. This made it possible to bring in a third partner, Energy Projects Plus (EPP), who would provide the expertise on energy prices, insulation and other technical matters. All these relationships were built up by mutually respectful conversations.

Parish Power has worked with schools and through them with parents who shared their own stories of strategies for managing budgets. Heating was followed by eating, and Parish Power moved into growing food and other plants, again working closely with schools and a wider group of partners, and also reclaiming an area of garden in the parish. A third stage, Hubs of Hope, is to develop an integrated approach to well-being in a project based in the church in St Helens where Kevin carries out his diaconal ministry, making the project part of the overall work of the parish. The project continues to grow.

## Church Action on Poverty

With other local people involved in Thrive, Kath uncovered huge dissatisfaction among customers with the actions of a high-cost lending company, Buy As You View (BAYV) – high credit charges, poor customer service, lack of transparency in what customers owed and so on. Based in Cardiff, BAYV sells TVs and other household appliances to over 100,000 people, and had something of a poor reputation for customer service. Most local projects would respond by encouraging customers to get help from the local CAB and seek redress on an individual basis. However, having been trained as a community leader through CAP's Changemakers Programme, Kath's response was to try to challenge the way the company itself operated – at the very top – by seeking a meeting with the boss of the company. With assistance from CAP's local worker, Kath and colleagues produced a spoof TV advert for BAYV highlighting the issue, which was watched by over 1,000 people on YouTube. It took considerable concerted action by CAP supporters to achieve a meeting with the managing director but in the end they managed. He accepted these concerns of his customers and acceded to all of Thrive's demands. Not only that – he agreed to work with Thrive to bring together a roundtable of high cost lenders along with the Office of Fair Trading to find a way forward. This roundtable, chaired by the Bishop John Packer, spent several months developing an industry-wide code for responsible lending, which benefits up to 325,000 customers of high-cost lending companies.

## Greenwich Peninsula Chaplaincy

By the early 2000s a combination of development projects, including the Millennium Dome, began the transformation of poisoned wasteland into a new community of 30,000 residents, 20,000 daily visitors, 20,000 people working in office blocks, the O2 and retail outlets, and a higher education college staff and students. As no space was allocated for religious use, the faith communities either had to resign themselves to a vast new community without visible religious activity or work to make something happen.

In March 2003, initiated by the Team Rector of East Greenwich, there was a meeting between the developers, Greenwich Borough Council and the faith communities. The faith communities offered to establish a multifaith team of workplace chaplains. In return, the developers and Greenwich Borough Council offered to provide a large permanent building for the faith communities to use together, an offer

> *Workplace chaplains are sometimes asked: 'So you are taking God into work?' to which they are likely to answer: 'No, I am going there to see what he is doing.'*
> Randell Moll, letter to the *Church Times* 17 April 2015

subsequently enshrined in the Section 106 agreement attached to the planning agreement. Over the next three years, the Greenwich Peninsula Chaplaincy was formed as a charitable trust, the first team of chaplains set to work on the O2 construction site and, when the O2 opened, they started work in its restaurants, cafés and bars. They now work in the O2, on construction sites, in ASDA, the borough's police stations and the College. In 2010 a temporary prayer space opened, open for three hours a day, staffed by volunteer welcomers and used by a variety of faith communities for their own religious activities. The chaplaincy provided several chaplains for the Olympic and Paralympic Games in 2012 and a large team of trained welcomers kept the Prayer Space open throughout the Games. Now the multifaith team of chaplains serve in a variety of workplaces. A prayer space is still open for three hours every day, staffed by volunteers and used by a variety of local faith communities – Muslim, Baha'i and three Christian denominations – for their own activities.

## Cardinal Hume Centre

The Cardinal Hume Centre (CHC) was founded by Cardinal Basil Hume in 1986 to help some of the poorest people he saw living in London – homeless young people sleeping rough and families in bed and breakfast accommodation. Today the centre

71

still supports homeless young people and badly housed families, alongside people from the local community in Westminster with little or no income who face multiple challenges in turning their lives around. The aim is to help people gain the skills they need to break out of poverty and build better lives, focusing on four major issues: housing; income; education and skills; formal immigration status. Partner organizations complement CHC services to offer a holistic approach to need, sharing the (limited) space, which reinforces the centre's role as a local hub.

Its foundation and ethos are unambiguously Catholic with a Benedictine flavour, but members of staff with no faith formation are able to identify with key concepts such as welcoming the stranger, providing a place of sanctuary and offering non-judgemental hospitality. Although many if not most of its supporters and friends are faith-motivated, the work of CHC takes place in a largely secular context. Of the CHC's active funding partnerships, none are with organizations that are overtly faith-based, and its committed volunteers come from many backgrounds.

CHC is an active member of CSAN (see above) and enjoys good working relationships with ecumenical allies such as Housing Justice and Church Action on Poverty as well as many local networks. CHC relates to many charities and bodies that are (multi-) faith-based or are secular, and the centre plays host to a wide variety of organizations. Its flexible approach has enabled it to respond creatively to changing needs and deliver services more effectively.

## Portsmouth Council for Social Responsibility

In addition to engaging with a range of social issues, over recent years the Anglican Diocese of Portsmouth has adapted its long-standing Council for Social Responsibility (CSR) and adopted a socially enterprising approach committed to supporting local churches in responding to their rapidly changing local communities: 'As the church and the wider society has changed, so has the work that it is undertaking, along with its emphasis and the language we use.' The Rapid Parish Development Programme (RPDP) is for local parishes considering building projects to open up their churches to the community. RPDP helps parishes develop an understanding of local dynamics and opportunities, identify necessary elements for their schemes and involve key stakeholders and funders in their vision and objectives. This approach is now attracting considerable interest in other dioceses. At a time when church growth is high on the agenda of many churches, examination of a 'social growth' model is a challenge to move beyond institutionally driven assumptions about mission and growth to grapple seriously with our present-day context.

> [I]n an unchurched (post-church?) society, an approach primarily based on 'proclaiming the good news' is neither credible nor sufficient. People who mostly do not share our experience and frame of reference first need to see the good news (a demonstration effect) and efforts to build God's Kingdom here and now – this is the only way to show, engage and involve them in transformation. (Nick Ralph 2015, p. 1)

## Doing good in small particulars

Bishop David Sheppard used to quote William Blake about the need to attend to 'small particulars'. He was underlining the importance of moving from broad principles to their implications, going beyond generalities to everyday nitty-gritty. These wide-ranging examples illustrate some of the many different ways in which people express their faith in faithful practice.

One common feature is respect for humanity. This is perhaps most obviously demonstrated by L'Arche, Hope+ and the Places of Welcome, but in other examples too it is often evident that the roles of helper and helped become blurred. Helpers gain as much as they give from the relationship. Service users go on to become volunteers. Recognition of the uniqueness of each individual and sharing are key.

Seeking to respond to the immediate context is another characteristic. This might be through adapting the church buildings to enable greater integration with the local community, as in Longbenton. It might be to contribute to community building in the Greenwich Peninsula through multifaith action to serve residents, visitors and workers in this newly created place. It might be to address problems such as food poverty or homelessness or debt

> He who would do good to another must do it in minute particulars.
> William Blake

or asylum. In all cases there is awareness of the importance of looking beyond the presenting problem. Invariably other needs must be addressed before the person can flourish. 'Looking beyond' for Hope+ Foodbank, for example, entails dealing with trauma as well as material needs, whereas for Church Action on Poverty it means addressing the practices of loan companies that exacerbate debt problems.

A third thread is acknowledgement of the need for flexibility and ongoing review. For CHC, partnership with others has enabled a more imaginative and holistic response to needs. Parish Power is trying to combine encouraging care for creation with the doorstep issue of coping with energy prices. The CSR in Portsmouth – an organization whose roots go back nearly 100 years – is developing innovative ways for churches to break out of institution-bound thinking to tailor their mission to their particular parish.

## Facing the challenge of change

> I prefer a Church which is bruised and dirty because it has been out on the streets, rather than a Church which is unhealthy from being confined and from clinging to its own security. (Pope Francis 2013, paragraph 49)

> Our research suggests that this tradition of active, socially engaged evangelicalism is alive and well, and continuing to make a significant impact on the life and welfare of British society in the twenty-first century. (Greg Smith 2015b, p. 57)

Initiating and sustaining projects will always be accompanied by challenges. For many – as in the wider voluntary and community sector – resources are diminishing in the current economic context at the same time as there is a rising tide of need, especially among already vulnerable groups in already deprived neighbourhoods. Services are shrinking and eligibility criteria are becoming stricter. In some spheres, voluntary organizations are being asked to take on responsibilities that previously lay with the public sector. Some will hesitate because they do not want to seem to collude with the creeping dismantlement of social protection. In any case, these opportunities to become more involved in delivering services mainly come without the necessary resources. The risk, therefore, is of already thinly stretched pools of paid workers and volunteers becoming even more overextended. And undertaking contracts entails a huge amount of time and energy and potential tensions between the requirements of the contracting body and the practice values of the organization concerned, affecting, for instance, the amount of time that can be given to individuals or the comprehensiveness of the service provided.

A CUF survey examining the impact of the economic climate on community organizations in the most deprived areas of England found that organizations were having to use a range of survival strategies to increase service provision in response to surging need.

One side effect was their increased willingness to collaborate and work in partnership with others (CUF 2012). Securing allies and finding ways of working in partnership – whether with other Christians, people of other faiths or secular partners – is another challenge. But doctrinal or other differences are not necessarily impediments to working together for social justice. Considering who else is out there can be a dimension of deciding – or not – on a project in the first place. If others are already active in a particular sphere, why not either co-operate or stand back rather than seeming to set up in competition? It is not always necessary or appropriate either to be in the lead or to 'brand' everything.

These – and more – were the sorts of issues that emerged when the T4CG research asked people engaged in social action about critical factors, both positive and negative. Recurring points mentioned were:

- Include 'beneficiaries' in shaping and running the programme – put the tools and skills for change into the hands of people directly affected.
- Ensure projects are serving a genuine need, not just imposing models from elsewhere.
- Don't reinvent the wheel and duplicate services already being delivered.
- Don't be afraid of failure – be willing to take a risk.
- Avoid silo thinking and the fear that working with people from a different Christian or faith background will dilute what is being done.
- Collaboration is a means not an end in itself – focus on a shared passion for social justice as the key starting point.
- Avoid the kind of competition between churches and

organizations – for funding or clients – that diminishes effectiveness.

- Establish clear shared objectives and clear expectations of what each partner will contribute.
- Goodwill alone is not enough for consistency and quality of service delivery – formalize collaborative structures through, for example, a memorandum of understanding.
- Develop good relationships outside of the church, such as with schools, CAB, social workers.
- Don't stand still – continue to grow and develop in the service provided as leaders and as organizations.
- Be aware of capacity issues and the associated ethical questions.

## Any ingredients worth bottling?

> *I think what we would feel is that there is an impetus to be a witness to our faith ... Intrinsically we are doing what we are doing because we believe in the common good and human dignity. So we act that out in what we are doing.*
> Helen O'Brien, CSAN, interview

Another question in the research was about what it is that distinguishes faith-based projects. Some of the answers resonated with what was said in the last chapter about faithful capital. On the one hand, faith groups have practical contributions to make through their resources of people and buildings, but perhaps more importantly through their long-standing presence in, and reach into, some of the communities that agencies often find hard to reach. On the other hand, there is the vision and faith that motivates people and provides a basis for their organizations and projects. Niall Cooper of Church Action on Poverty talked of the influence of biblical teaching:

> In theological terms all people are made in the image of God, and all people have the spark of creativity, have human agency and when those are denied to them, then they are denied what it is to be fully human. That's ultimately what all the stuff about empowerment is about. It's about enabling people to exercise their God-given talents to live lives that are dignified and able to live lives to the full. And that requires an analysis of institutions as well as individuals – institutional sin, like the idea of institutional racism – it's when institutions actually oppress or exercise power over people in ways which diminish their humanity and their dignity. That is an injustice and it has to be the role of communities to name that and to challenge it. (Niall Cooper, interview)

A strong justice theme also came through the responses. Steve McGanity from St Andrew's Church, Clubmoor, which has such a huge community focus, is inspired by the emphasis on social justice running through the Old Testament:

> Huge chunks of the Bible are about God's heart for the poor or as David Sheppard would say 'God's bias for the poor', which is a phrase that has stuck with me. I can't read the Bible without seeing that. For me personally that has been quite strong ... So particularly Isaiah 49 or 58, 35 and 61, they've been passages that have been important in different ways in our history, certainly in the early history of what we started to do. The passages that are all about restoration and about ruins in the desert have been images and passages that have been quite strong for us.

However, there were also cautionary words about claiming too much distinctiveness and certainly against any hint of triumphalism, not least because many Christians called to work in secular organizations are also inspired by biblical principles.

## Reflecting God's greater hospitality

Rowan Williams (2004) talks about the Church being a place of transforming encounter, an assembly of people having their relationships and lives transfigured by the presence of Jesus. It is an event before it is an institution: 'not an association of people who happen to have the same ideas' – well, as an Anglican I can certainly confirm it's not that – 'but the beginning of God's reclaiming of the territory of human life and not just human life either, God's reclaiming of creation as his own . . . The church is the name we give to those networks, those places, those which embody the event of the new creation. The church is what happens when Jesus is there, there received and recognized.' The Resourcing Christian Community Action study traced a wide range of theological themes threading through the sample of projects that showed how they *are* church and how they can inform other dimensions of church life.

- *Caring* featured in them all because the motivation came from the fact that people cared about others, and the value attached to each and every individual was demonstrated through that care.
- *Hospitality* was another theme that was often present but perhaps seen most strikingly in relation to asylum seekers and refugees.
- *Presence* – being there – was another theological strand. Very often the church project was the most long-standing one in the community as others came and went. It was the 'enduring, faithful presence'.
- *Liberation* was another theme: projects often struggling to help people escape the shackles represented by their different problems, whether poverty, unemployment, homelessness, broken relationships or isolation.
- Yet another strand was *Inclusion*: not just that social

inclusion was a goal of some projects but also that they were not making a strict divide between doer and done-to. As already mentioned, clients sometimes go on to be volunteers; but in any case, staff and volunteers recognize the mutuality involved and how they benefit from the relationships formed.

- **Creation** was an obvious theme in relation to some of the environmental and climate-change projects, which also extend the vision of interdependence globally and to future generations.

- Finally, **Justice** was a theme among projects: speaking out about injustice and inequality, and awareness that, although there are opportunities to be commissioned to deliver caring services, it is important not to become so enmeshed in 'the system' that you lose the capacity to speak truth to power.

> For most who offer hospitality the experience is deeply enriching as well as quite demanding. Strangers rarely bring only their needs; within the hospitality relationship, hosts often experience profound blessing. Acts of hospitality participate in and reflect God's greater hospitality and therefore hold some connection to the divine, to holy ground.
>
> Christine Pohl 1999, p. 13

'Speaking truth to power' brings us to another role for the wider Church and its leaders. At project level there can be tensions between the pastoral and prophetic roles; between meeting needs and speaking out about the impact of the economy and public policies on vulnerable people and communities. These projects are trying to foster strong social bonds in interpersonal relationships. However, it is equally important to seek economic and social policies incorporating such bonds, based on the principles of human dignity, solidarity, subsidiarity and an 'option for the poor'. This is the subject of the next chapter.

# 6
## Voices in the Public Square

*The Christian principles from which we start require that we should approach the whole social problem and every part of it from the standpoint of the true interest of men and women as persons.*

William Temple 1958, p. 206

*Christian believers in every age have to ask with proper humility: 'What is God saying to us in this situation?' and that question leads to a more general one: 'What can we trace of God's hand in the events of our time?'*

V. A. Demant 1952, p. 177

### A forum for moral discourse?

The age of Christendom has passed. The Church is now at the margins. This may feel intimidating and – literally – edgy, but it is where we should be. In the words of Bishop Paul Bayes, speaking at his first Diocesan Synod in Liverpool in March 2015:

> We are called at this time to be on the edge and underneath. No longer – if we ever were – to be in the middle and at the top. We are called to stand where our Lord stood and where the first disciples stood, on the edge of our society and underneath, oriented to the unchanging love of God for the poor, extending the table of the poor Christ into every street, every workplace and every home. Only there – only if we stoop low enough – can we see the face of God.

If it is only there that we can see the face of God, it is also only there that we can get a fresh perspective on our society and bring any distinctive voice.

Duncan Forrester suggested 25 years ago that the Church needs to rediscover itself as a forum for moral discourse. 'The day of pre-packaged answers and "moral instruction" is long past. We now realize more fully than in the past the increasing complexity of many modern ethical dilemmas and hence the impossibility of simple, rule-of-thumb solutions' (Forrester 1989, p. 96). If that was true then, it is more so now. It calls for continuing, open, participative and frank engagement with issues and reflection on public policy that is realistic, theologically serious and cogently argued. It also means taking chances, being imaginative, countercultural and adventurous, with the accompanying risk of making mistakes.

## Kingdom building

Speaking out on economic and social structures that present a challenge to Christian notions of justice, hospitality and reverence for creation is an imperative. To remain silent denotes consent and gives implicit support to the status quo. And the stress is on kingdom building, not protecting the interests of the Church. The challenge is how to speak and act in the public arena *as* the Church, proclaiming the kingdom rather than defending the interests of an institution; showing that it is not just one social institution among many but the sign and foretaste of the kingdom of God (Forrester 1989, p. 52).

> *Embracing the common good also impels us to move beyond the party political agenda to consider the kind of society we wish to live in.*
> Andrew Bradstock, in Sagovsky and McGrail 2015, p. 16

As earlier chapters have already indicated, the Church 'speaks' in many ways: through its members in their lay or civil roles; through the outreach of local churches; through Christian groups; through the organization of its institutional life. The local level is usually mainly about confronting the consequences of social, economic and environmental problems and finding ways of making a difference. But that experience feeds into addressing the systemic issues that lie behind these symptoms.

An integral element of Catholic Social Teaching has been the appraisal of economic systems and, as in other strands of Christian thought, there is suspicion both of a highly centralized

> *No one can give a definitive social theology, because it is continually forged in interaction with the world.*
>
> Alan Suggate, in Brown 2014, p. 28

state and of unbridled free markets. However, while the extremes may be rejected, there are many possible positions in between. How then do we read the world and the signs of the times? How do we read the Bible in the context of our culture and situation? What does it mean to be salt and light today? Every age poses new questions about what we should really worry about, which trends we should support and which resist. It is worth pausing here to try to capture some background features of our context today. As we look around, what do we see?

## A runaway world

In his 1999 Reith lectures, Anthony Giddens talked about us living in a 'runaway world'. He quoted one Archbishop Wulfstan preaching in York in 1014 saying 'The world is in a rush, and is getting close to its end'; and as Giddens said, it is easy to imagine the same sentiments today. But he also asked if today's hopes and anxieties are any different, and his answer is yes, they are, because we are facing not just external forces-of-nature risks but also what has been called manufactured risk, created by the impact of our developing knowledge on the world. As Giddens puts it:

> At a certain point ... very recently in historical terms, we started worrying less about what nature can do to us, and more about what we have done to nature. This marks the transition from the predominance of external risk to that of manufactured risk. (Giddens 1999, p. 26)

Perhaps those of us in richer parts of the world assume that we are less vulnerable to traditional risks. But no matter where we live and regardless of how wealthy or privileged we are, we face risk situations – from global warming and ecological risks to the uncertainties of the global economy and all their effects on our political and social institutions. We are increasingly conscious of the consequences of human intervention, even to the point of recognizing that much of what used to be natural is no longer natural and that it is hard to know where the one ends and the other begins.

One aspect of this new manufactured risk is the transformation of world economies by technological advances. Capital moves freely around the world. Transnational corporations have turnovers exceeding some national economies. It is argued (Giddens 1998, pp. 31–2) that this shrinking of the world has:

- 'pulled away' from the nation state, reducing its power to manage the economy;
- 'pushed down', bringing new demands and possibilities for more local identities, whether these are based on geography or other interests;
- 'squeezed sideways', creating new economic/cultural regions cross-cutting nation state boundaries.

We only have to look at the financial crisis of 2008, the demands for greater devolution and the realignment of different countries and blocs to recognize these features. Globalization has also paved the way for the mass movement of people around the world – inward and outward migration and, therefore, more ethnically diverse places.

Another key feature of our current economic way of life is that it is based on consumption and the circulation of commodities. Modern capitalism requires an array of consumers whose tastes and preferences can be organized and segmented. It has gone beyond satisfying material needs. The market responds to people's tastes, wants and demands and organizes itself to trade on impulses and insecurities. It is a cultural as well as an economic process, which is all about branding: brand as products that are not commodities but concepts; brand as experience; brand as lifestyle. So there is no limit to consumer demand. Nor does it end there. Consumer goods have become the model for social goods – from water and energy to pensions, health and education. 'Choice' has become a key word in relation to medical treatment and schools, and again we see tensions between individual interests and the common good. There are even approaches to politics now that can be described as consumerist – perhaps not surprising with so many pressures towards self-interested choices.

An increasingly prominent and disturbing development has been growing inequality. A report by the New Economics Foundation (NEF) finds a link between this and the deregulation and expansion of the financial sector. The penetration of profit-led motives into more and more areas of society, as well as shifts in economic activity, have seen power move from public to private interests. The NEF report calls this 'financialization'. Corporate profit-seeking through commercial activities, such as producing goods or providing services, is being overtaken by seeking returns through financial trading and increasing returns for shareholders. The growth of the sector is marked by the creation of new financial instruments and increased economic transactions between countries, which in turn require state support to cover the risks to the rest of the economy. An accompanying trend has been the declining share of wages to total income as measured by gross domestic product (GDP), and the rising share of profits by private business owners, shareholders and financial investors. There has also been growing inequality in the distribution of wages over the past 25 years. For those at the top, pay has escalated, whereas those on average or below average earnings have seen only very modest rises.

> *Just as any revolution eats its children, unchecked market fundamentalism can devour the social capital essential for the long-term dynamism of capitalism itself. All ideologies are prone to extremes. Capitalism loses its sense of moderation when the belief in the power of the market enters the realm of faith. Market fundamentalism ... contributed directly to the financial crisis and the associated erosion of social capital.*
>
> Oxfam 2014, p. 55, quoting Mark Carney,
> Governor of the Bank of England

The converse of this is that economic inequality is one of the forces that contributes to financial instability. There are a number of drivers: weak demand and a drop in consumption; higher household debt often with very high interest charges; debt-led growth at a national level where inflows of financial capital are not balanced by exports; increasingly risky financial activities encouraged by those at the top end of the income scale who can afford to take such risks.

## Not by bread alone

Richard Wilkinson and Kate Pickett (2010) talk about 'material success but social failure'. They discuss the relationship between inequality and a wide range of social problems and underline how everyone is damaged by inequality because these problems impact on communities at large and on public spending. The operation of markets in the context of globalization leads inevitably both to extreme concentrations of wealth and increasingly irrational outcomes in the way funds are dispersed to combat threats or promote public goods. 'The widening gap between the rich and poor, in wealth and income, is bad for everyone – even the super wealthy, unless, that is, they never want to leave their fortified, hermetically sealed, lavishly appointed bunkers' (Robert Peston, BBC News, 19 January 2015). In other words there are many instrumental reasons to combat inequality. But the argument against is more than a pragmatic one: such inequality offends against any notion of human dignity and individual worth.

Richard Layard, the economist, has written about 'happiness' and the fact that increasing prosperity has been accompanied not by greater contentment but by growing anxiety and discontent. Once basic needs are met, income rises are not mirrored by equivalent increases in well-being – not least because our norms and expectations shift, constantly adapting to higher and higher consumer standards which we then require to sustain our happiness. This also underlines that poverty is a relative concept. When, for example, people say there is no poverty today compared with the 1930s, they are focusing on the material and failing to take account of the social, psychological and relational dimensions of poverty. But even for those not remotely disadvantaged, the seeming assumption that material goods and retail therapy can cure all ills is very evidently misguided.

The former Chief Rabbi, Jonathan Sacks posed the sorts of

questions we should ask of any economic system and, notably, he did this at the peak of the boom rather than with the hindsight of recession:

> Does it enhance human dignity? Does it create self-respect? Does it encourage creativity? Does it allow everyone to participate in the material blessings of this created world? Does it sustain a climate of equal regard – for employees as well as employers, the poor no less than the rich? Does it protect the vulnerable and help those in need to escape the trap of need? Does it ensure that no one lacks the means for a dignified existence? Do those who succeed share their blessings with those who have less? Does the economic system strengthen the bonds of human solidarity? And does it know its limits – does it recognize that its values are not the only values, that there is more to life than a perpetual striving after wealth, the market is not the only mechanism of distribution, and that an economic system is a means not an end? (Sacks 2001, p. 23)

## Stewards for the future

> If we lived rationally, we should be taking instant action about those features of our present life that are making the human future more and more precarious. (Rowan Williams 2012, p. 175)

If faith in debt-led growth and the lure of consumerism is damaging here and now, how much more will it have destructive consequences both for less-developed countries now and for the whole earth in the future. We have behaved as though resources are infinitely expandable or that, even if they are not, technology will come to the rescue. A major cost of economic growth is the diminution of natural resources. The macro-economy is expanding into the ecosystem, displacing what was there before whether through the destruction of the natural habitats of other species, the uprooting of people to make way for industrial or technological development, increasing pollution or climate change.

> *Globalisation ... makes us much more aware of the togetherness of the whole human family. We really are mutually dependent. We are all in it together. In an even more dramatic way, the scare about climate change and environmental pollution has opened our eyes to yet another level of who we are as 'together people' ... not just bound together with other human persons. We are also bound together with all living creatures and the whole of creation.*
>
> Kevin Kelly 2012, p. 148

Rowan Williams suggests that there are Christian reasons for regarding ecology 'as essentially a matter of justice for the human as well as the non-human world' (2012, p. 176), arguing that our short-termism is a result of a consumerist attitude to creation rather than understanding creation as gift. Instead of thinking it is just there for our use, we should use creation as a means of sharing the divine generosity with others (p. 177).

## Impacts

The evolution of Catholic Social Teaching has often been in response to particular developments or circumstances. For example, the founding document, *Rerum novarum* in 1891, was prompted by the growing disparity between capital and labour arising from the industrial revolution. The notable resurgence in interest in the common good in the UK over the past few years is perhaps not surprising, therefore, coinciding as it does with a period of austerity measures. A more blatant gulf between rich and poor has caused people to question underpinning political values, sharpen the critique of individualism and consumerism that affects us all and challenge the primacy of economic growth as a political goal.

The section above painted in some of the backcloth, but how does it appear in close-up, in the foreground of people's lives?

- Almost one-third (33 per cent) of the UK population (approximately 19.3 million people) experienced poverty in at least one year between 2010 and 2013, whereas across the EU as a whole, 25 per cent of people were in poverty at least once during that period (Office for National Statistics 2015, p. 1).

- Tables 1 and 2 show the Households Below Average Income figures for relative low income and absolute low income before and after housing costs and for different population groups in urban and rural areas for 2011/12 (Defra 2013, p. 86). 'Relative' is in comparison to median income in the current year; 'absolute' is compared with median income in 2010–11.

- Rural poverty is often wrongly overlooked because it is less concentrated, but incomes can be lower and living costs higher than in urban areas. The seasonal nature of industries such as agriculture and tourism mean insecure and short-term employment. Several factors combine to put costs up: high private-sector rents, high energy prices, the cost of transport and longer distances to cheaper food suppliers.

> *Research shows that people in rural areas typically need to spend 10–20 per cent more than people in urban areas to reach a minimum acceptable living standard. These higher costs mean a single person living in a village needs to earn at least 50 per cent above the minimum wage to make ends meet.*
>
> Smith, Davis and Hirsch 2010, p. 49

*Table 1: Relative low income, percentage, 2011/12*

| | Rural | | Urban | |
|---|---|---|---|---|
| | Before housing costs | After housing costs | Before housing costs | After housing costs |
| Households | 13 | 15 | 18 | 23 |
| Working-age people | 11 | 15 | 16 | 23 |
| Children | 11 | 17 | 19 | 30 |
| Pensioners | 14 | 12 | 17 | 14 |

*Table 2: Absolute low income, percentage, 2011/12*

| | Rural | | Urban | |
|---|---|---|---|---|
| | Before housing costs | After housing costs | Before housing costs | After housing costs |
| Households | 15 | 17 | 19 | 24 |
| Working-age people | 12 | 15 | 17 | 24 |
| Children | 12 | 18 | 21 | 32 |
| Pensioners | 15 | 14 | 19 | 16 |

- Around 40 per cent of black and Asian ethnic minorities live in poverty: about twice the rate for white people. Research shows ethnicity affects levels and experiences of poverty, but how the two are linked is complex and not yet well understood (Joseph Rowntree Foundation 2014).
- In addition to myths about the motives and entitlements of asylum seekers, there are frequently misconceptions about numbers. At the end of 2014 the population of refugees,

pending asylum cases and stateless persons made up just 0.24 per cent of the UK population (UNHCR 2014).

> *A refugee is a person who: 'owing to a well-founded fear of being persecuted for reasons of race, religion, nationality, membership of a particular social group, or political opinion, is outside the country of his nationality, and is unable to or, owing to such fear, is unwilling to avail himself of the protection of that country'.*
>
> UN Convention relating to the status of refugees, 1951
>
> *An asylum seeker is someone who has lodged an application for protection on the basis of the Refugee Convention or Article 3 of the ECHR.*

- Half of the 13 million people living in poverty in the UK today are part of a working family. Between 2008 and 2013 the national minimum wage fell in real terms by £13 per week for someone working full time. The increase in numbers living below a minimum income standard can be explained more by stagnant wages and cuts to in-work benefits than people having less work. This means the risk of a family falling short of a minimum income standard can increase despite their work status remaining the same (McInnes et al. 2014).
- There is a wide gap between housing supply and projected new household formation. Since 2008 only just over 100,000 homes per year have been developed in England. The target needed for new demand and tackling the backlog is 250,000 (Heath 2014, p. 1). During the 2014/15 financial year, 54,430 households were accepted by local authorities in England as being owed the main homelessness duty. This is an increase of 4 per cent from 2013/14 and continued a trend of steady increases from 2009/10 (Department of Communities and Local Government 2015).

- Some 2.28m households experience fuel poverty in England; the highest rates are in the north (Joseph Rowntree Foundation 2015).

- The removal of the spare room subsidy ('bedroom tax') that came into effect in 2013 reduces Housing Benefit for working-age tenants in properties with more rooms than the size criteria of the Department for Work and Pensions (DWP) state that they need: by 14 per cent for one extra room or 25 per cent for two or more. Over 500,000 households were affected – over 11 per cent of all social tenancies. Nearly half had lived in their property for over ten years. About two-thirds of those affected were disabled. Lack of available smaller homes limits the number of households able to move. Some affected claimants moved to the private rented sector where rents – and therefore housing benefit – tend to be higher. Rents in London are not an affordable option. After five months nearly 60 per cent of those affected were having to cut down on other household essentials and/or borrow money, but even so they had still fallen behind with their rent to a greater or lesser extent (Clarke et al. 2014).

> *One man in Birmingham who made a mistake on his application for Jobseeker's Allowance (JSA) received no money for twelve weeks, during which he was seen rummaging in the bins behind a chip shop. When the owner got fed up with this and phoned the police, the man was arrested for trespassing.*
> Evidence Review of the All Party Parliamentary Inquiry into Hunger in the UK, December 2014

- The Trussell Trust reports that from April 2014 to end March 2015 over one million people in crisis received three days' emergency food and support from their foodbanks, not counting distribution by the many foodbanks not registered with the Trust or other forms of assistance such as soup kitchens, lunch clubs and food parcels. Food poverty can be about more than shortage of money; it may be about access to affordable food or the lack of cooking facilities or adequate food storage.

- In 2014 one million benefit sanctions were imposed, stopping payments usually for a month, occasionally for up to three years. The most common reason is the claimant being late for, or missing, an appointment. Sanctions disproportionately affect young people, homeless people, young people leaving care, single parents and those with long-term illness or mental health problems (DWP).

> For the past year I served as the President of the Methodist Conference. This gave me the opportunity to meet and talk to people all around Britain. From Cornwall to Shetland, from Lancashire to Lincolnshire, in urban and rural areas, I met Christians who are collecting for foodbanks, or working in foodbanks. In every area I asked the same two questions: Do you have a foodbank here? Have you seen an increased need for it? Wherever I travelled the answers to both questions was 'yes'. I wasn't hearing about small increases in need; rather I was hearing about huge leaps in demand and foodbanks that were struggling to keep up. I was hearing about generosity of giving in terms of time and food. I was hearing about, and talking with, people who were falling into unmanageable debt for the first time in their lives.
>
> Foreword by Ruth Gee, President of the Methodist Conference 2013/14, to Joint Public Issues Team and Church Action on Poverty 2014

- Income and employment differences are linked with wide variations in mortality and morbidity rates. In 2013 the North

East had a 12 per cent higher mortality rate than the rest of the country. Contrasts can be seen within local authority areas (Office for National Statistics). The Life Expectancy Wirral project was developed by the Diocese of Chester in response to people on the Mersey side of the Wirral dying on average nearly 12 years younger than those living on the Dee side.

> When the Pew Research Center's Global Attitudes Project asked respondents in 2014 about 'the greatest danger to the world', it found that in the United States and Europe 'concerns about inequality trump all other dangers'.
>
> Anthony Atkinson 2015, p. 1

- Such health inequalities stem from inequalities in the determinants of health, such as poverty and poor housing, and are then exacerbated when social security provision and other safety nets are weakened.

> ... the material and moral interests of the dominant section of British society and the prevailing ideas of the age go comfortably hand in hand. In the words of the old soldiers' song:
>
> It's the same the whole world over,
> It's the poor wot gets the blame,
> It's the rich wot gets the gravy.
>
> The last of those two lines are certainly true of Britain today, but views obviously differ about whether or not they also amount to 'a bleedin' shame'.
>
> Anthony King 2015, p. 142

- The poorest places and the poorest people are being the hardest hit. London boroughs (31.4 per cent), the North

East (26.7 per cent) and the North West (25.7 per cent) have seen the largest average cuts in spending per person between 2009–10 and 2014–15 (Innes and Tetlow 2015).

- Those least able to cope with service withdrawal bear the brunt of service reduction. Social care spending (combining children and adult services) rose in real terms in the least deprived categories (by £28 per head or 8 per cent) while falling strongly in the most/more deprived categories (by £65 per head or 14 per cent). With one-third of disabled adults already living in poverty, the most disabled people and those needing social care have been hit up to 19 times harder by cuts than others (Centre for Welfare Reform).

- Research by PwC has found that the average UK household will owe close to £10,000 in personal loans, credit cards and overdrafts by the end of 2016. Total outstanding non-mortgage borrowing grew by nearly £20 billion or 9 per cent in 2014, to reach £239 billion (PwC 2015).

- Another face of debt is revealed by the Money Advice Trust. The National Debtline saw a 140 per cent rise in the number seeking help with household debt between 2007 and 2013. There was a shift in the type of debt problem as a result of rising bills and falling incomes. Fewer reported problems with traditional credit products; more wanted advice on debts concerning energy, water, telephone, council tax and catalogue shopping bills. The Children's Society found that 1.6 million children live in households that have faced council tax debt, with profound effects on the children's lives causing them anxiety and depression and fear of bailiffs coming to call (Capron and Ayre 2015).

> *Calls about council tax arrears almost doubled 2007–14; energy bills were up by 171 per cent; phone bill arrears up 230 per cent; water bill arrears up 305 per cent.*
> Money Advice Trust 2014

## A calling to transform

> The age of incarnation embodies the transition from the age of atonement, regarding life on earth as journeying through a vale of tears to an eternal home, to regarding life on earth as a calling to transform God's world for the better (John Atherton 2000, p. 79).

The last chapter discussed the pastoral or service role of faith groups. It is the existence of Christian social and community action in all parts of society that gives the Church the authority to speak with integrity in the public arena with and for those who would not otherwise have a voice. This exposure to people and communities enables it to take the pulse of society. In seeing and listening, it becomes apparent that sticking plasters are not enough. Vital as it is, social action must not get in the way of social justice. But seeking justice is hard because it means challenging the 'system' and the vested interests of those who benefit from it.

Duncan Forrester asked for whom the Church speaks. There is always a danger of surrendering any claim to speak into the public square for a variety of reasons: if the Church colludes in the 'privatization' of faith by being willing to be confined to the private and individual; if it is preoccupied with institutional disagreements or protecting institutional interests; and/or if it lacks confidence over whether Christianity has anything distinctive to say.

> The Church should speak out, whatever the cost, when constrained to do so by the gospel. It speaks to announce the kingdom, to proclaim the gospel, to affirm the justice of God, not to defend its own institutional interests.
>
> Duncan Forrester 1989, p. 54

In 1985 South African theologians and church leaders produced a typology of theology in the *Kairos Document*, which is still relevant. In the South African context of the time, *state* theology amounted to a theological justification of the status quo, including its racism. *Church* theology made some limited and cautious criticism of apartheid but proclaimed 'a cheap grace, reconciliation without repentance, peace before justice'. Determination to be even-handed meant it stated nothing clearly but rather nailed its colours to the fence (Forrester 1989, p. 59). The *Kairos Document* called instead for

> a response from Christians that is biblical, spiritual, pastoral and, above all, prophetic. It is not enough in these circumstances to repeat generalised Christian principles. We need a bold and incisive response that is prophetic because it speaks to the particular circumstances of this crisis. (Kairos Theologians 1985, p. 4)

We might all agree with this for our circumstances, but with the proviso that, as Keith Clements points out, the adjective 'prophetic' has to mean more than just any outspoken comment on contemporary society. Prophetic witness must be strengthened and given content. Clements cites the examples of Bishop George Bell during the Second World War speaking out against the saturation bombing of civilians in Germany, and Martin Luther King's fight for racial justice in the USA. In both cases their spoken witness was authenticated by costly actions. 'But "prophetic" as applied to lesser mortals can too readily be a euphemism for a strident exercise in denunciation which achieves little beyond a self-righteous glow of satisfaction for the speaker' (Clements 2011, p. 81).

Another pertinent question is *to* whom the Church is speaking. To make a difference, statements need to be targeted effectively. They may be addressed primarily to church members to challenge them to examine their views and responsibilities or alert them to particular issues. Pre-election and pastoral letters from bishops come into this category. Or they may be addressed to decision-makers. In all cases, the key words are cogency, distinctiveness and consistency between what the Church is saying and its own organization and practice.

## Speaking into diversity

Rowan Williams has talked about two sorts of secularism. *Procedural* secularism pertains where the state defines its role as 'one of overseeing a variety of communities of religious conviction and, where necessary assisting them to keep the peace together' without giving any single community a legally favoured position. *Programmatic* secularism is where 'any and every public manifestation of any particular religious allegiance is to be ironed out' and clear public loyalty to the state must be 'unclouded by private convictions, and any sign of such private convictions are rigorously banned from public space'. The latter is problematic because it assumes only one sort of loyalty is possible. It reduces moral decisions to private, lifestyle choices and dilutes the possibility of challenging state rationality. Procedural secularism, however, poses no problems for Christians. A state that thinks of itself as a 'community of communities' and works with diverse religious groups 'to make best use of their resources for the common good and to minimize conflict' is one that sees its remit in more modest terms. It fits with 'a pluralist pattern of social life, with a lot of decentralized and co-operative activity'. It is also in accord with some of the most influential Christian political theologians, such as Augustine and Aquinas, whose ideas come close to this more pluralist ideal. 'Furthermore, this is not a vision that is the sole property of left or right in the contemporary context which is a good sign, if the Church is to continue to be what Karl Barth called an "unreliable ally" for any and every political system' (Williams 2012, p. 4).

The Christian contribution in the public square has

various dimensions: a voice bringing a different perspective; a conversation partner; a critical friend to the state and its laws.

> It asks about the foundations of what the state takes for granted and often challenges the shallowness of prevailing social morality; it pushes for change to make the state a little more like the community that it is itself representing, the Kingdom of God. It does not make the mistake of talking as though politics would bring the Kingdom into being on earth, but it continually seeks to make the promise of the Kingdom more concrete and visible in the common life of human beings, private and public. (Williams 2007)

## Conversation partners and unexpected allies

Being a conversation partner, undertaking ongoing dialogue and establishing shared values and common agendas can be more effective than one-off statements. Here are two examples of working with – sometimes unexpected – allies to achieve a more potent and compelling voice.

First an historic example. In 1982, after the disturbances in several British cities including Liverpool, Michael Heseltine had challenged the private sector to reverse its desertion of the inner cities. As Minister for Merseyside, he took directors from the City of London on a coach ride round parts of Merseyside, urging them to come and invest. When David Sheppard and Derek Worlock formed the Michaelmas Group, there seemed to have been little response to his challenge. The group began when the two church leaders invited senior managers from Merseyside businesses to meet in the Archbishop's House on Michaelmas Day 1984. It was agreed that 'those of us on the spot needed to see *our* responsibility and possibilities that lay with *us*, before asking outsiders to come and rescue us' (Sheppard 2002, p. 225). The Group was important in being 'a forum where senior decision-makers in the city could meet and talk about the Merseyside agenda in trust and security' (Furnival and Knowles 1998, p. 199). Later, when the broader scope for strategic discussion was curtailed by, for example, the abolition of Merseyside County Council, it became more of a behind-the-scenes enabling group. Its

> *There was learning on both sides. The extent and depth of poverty and its implications was conveyed and it became less easy for members to ignore. But the Bishops also both realized that they couldn't just articulate the needs of the poor because if they did, those trying to turn Liverpool around couldn't get any traction.*
> Roger Morris (Secretary to the Michaelmas Group), interview

hallmarks were trust and discretion. The presence of the two leaders was its distinctive ingredient because they were rooted in the area and identified closely with it, but were to some extent above the fray. However, other members brought knowledge and expertise and, as a result, the church leaders gained more insight into the operation of the commercial and public sectors.

An up-to-date example of dialogue is that of Christian Aid taking forward its concern about the disproportionate effects of climate change and company tax dodging on the world's poor. 'Surprising allies' were found among major players in the private sector. In the words of Christine Allen, the Christian Aid Director of Policy and Public Affairs:

> Here are two massive global issues – tax and climate change – with real impact on the lives of people in poverty around the world that also speak to the domestic, business agenda. If we take our time to think and analyse the problems we face, we can see the connections:
>
> - We often have more power than we realize, but we need to talk to the right people; working with others can really open doors.

- We can make surprising allies – non-governmental organizations (NGOs) and the private sector are increasingly working together – a long way from when people might have been described as being on the 'dark side' or just do-gooders running kitchen sink operations.
- Finding shared values – we have seen a sea change in Corporate Social Responsibility over the last ten years. For good businesses, it has moved into the boardroom. That is something to be proud of, and can create a massive agenda shift. So, many local organizations have strong and effective business links.
- We can share goals even if we come from different perspectives, so the potential for us to work together is higher than we think. (Christine Allen, interview)

## Two conversation models

There are other conversation models to enable exploration and learning about particular issues. Church Action on Poverty has considerable experience in organizing poverty hearings. Their purpose is to provide the opportunity for people with first-hand experience of poverty to speak for themselves while encouraging those with power, authority and different experiences to listen. Hearings are based on the belief that those in poverty are the real experts and that the rest of us need to listen and be prepared for what they say to surprise and shock us. Careful preparation is required to ensure that they are empowering not disabling, and that vulnerable people are afforded proper respect and dignity.

Together for the Common Good has produced a model for a 'Common Good Conversation' as a tool for tackling difficult issues by applying the principles of the common good and starting to work towards solutions. The aim is to reflect a wide range of possible viewpoints on the topic by bringing together people

with very different starting points and perspectives. The model was first tested in a conversation about housing among people in different positions in relation to the housing market. Two groups were involved: those participating in the initial conversation and 'listeners' – again from diverse backgrounds and potentially in a position to effect change – who later took part in break-out groups and wider discussion. A number of lessons emerged from the pilot. Setting the mood is important so that participants approach it in a spirit of openness, prepared to relinquish their prejudices and presuppositions. Language matters. The language of the common good is very powerful for such discourses, but also the language needs both to reflect the complexity of the topic and the diversity of participants. It must be suitable for building trust as well as candour, especially as it can be too easy in such situations to duck issues of personal responsibility. The subject should be one of immediate interest to those involved, not too general, well focused. Finally, in composing the group of attendees it may be significant to think about the future potential for networking and collaboration.

## Whose story?

There is no point in pretending that it is easy to reach consensus. Economic or social or community shocks in particular can provoke very varied reactions. This was illustrated at the end of the 1980s when the closure of the Birds Eye factory in Kirkby in Knowsley, Merseyside, was announced, with the loss of a thousand jobs. When the local Anglican clergy heard of the intended closure they felt they had to form a joint ecumenical response with their Roman Catholic and Methodist counterparts – not straightforward because existing links were personal and informal and not geared to such a sensitive undertaking. They all decided their clearest response should be liturgical and so they planned a day's vigil during Holy Week outside the factory gates to bear witness to the fact that their people were experiencing the same road of suffering and rejection that Christ had trodden. It was seen as an act of witness not blame. However, they also met both management and trade unions to hear their views and then shared this information together with their perceptions of the rights and wrongs.

Thus they prepared a joint statement, printed in the local paper and diocesan newspaper, in which they referred to the decision being based upon a system of values that idolized market forces and profit margins – fairly clear where their loyalties lay then. The Anglicans among them also proposed a motion to the Diocesan Synod asking the Church Commissioners disinvest its £21 million from the parent company, Unilever.

> The question at the heart of this debate was 'What should be the response of the Church to such situations?'. Whose story will take precedence? That of the managers who feel decisions are forced on them by reality of competition, or that of local residents who feel hurt and helpless? Perhaps it is inevitable and right that there are varied responses to a problem of such complexity and that part of the challenge for the Church is to contain this diversity in a loving and open way.
>
> Russell, Introduction to
> 'The Birds Eye Debate'. Papers given at
> Liverpool Diocesan Synod 7 October 1989

Meanwhile the church leaders were also active. On Good Friday they joined in a united procession for the Stations of the Cross, to be present with people at that time of hurt. But they were also seeking to bring the needs of the community to the attention of management at the highest level. Listening to managers who felt strongly that they had done all within their power to keep the Kirkby operation viable, the church leaders' efforts then concentrated on ensuring as humane a pull-out as possible and persuading the company to make some alternative investment – legacy funding – in the community.

All in all, a wonderfully Anglican story: pastoral care to the powerless and the powerful (though some would have disclaimed this description); prayer and protest; the generation of heat and the attempted generation of light. All these strands of activity may be seen as legitimate and it is appropriate to weave them together, albeit seemingly discordantly. But that also underestimates the real challenge that it was to the main church players in this drama to see themselves on the same side. In theory they may have recognized the validity of what others were doing; empathizing was another matter.

## Solidarity or neutrality?

If you are neutral in situations of injustice, you have chosen the side of the oppressor. If an elephant has its foot on the tail of a mouse and you say that you are neutral, the mouse will not appreciate your neutrality. (Desmond Tutu)

It is clear there can be diverse roles for leaders and others in the church: acting as honest broker, advocate or challenger. Clifford Longley, in *The Worlock Archive*, refers to Archbishop Derek Worlock as 'a highly political churchman'.

In matters touching politics and society, Derek Worlock gradually established himself as one of the most thoughtful and outspoken Church leaders of his generation, of any denomination. That is not to acquit him of *naïveté*, nor to say he was right about everything (or even most things). But he was identified with this issue, and glad to be. Given his ministry in Liverpool, this was not inappropriate. If any city did, this one needed some standing up for. And yet, and yet ... (Longley 2000, p. 313)

The question Longley leaves dangling here is whether such partisanship – by David Sheppard as well as Derek Worlock – came at the cost that such an approach could readily generate or reinforce a victim mentality, a mindset that sapped morale and energy. Longley questions the comprehensiveness of Worlock's analysis of the social disintegration he saw occurring in Liverpool neighbourhoods. He also suspects that such perceptions were tinged with 'liberal guilt', so that 'he ignores some factors that are present out of a decent and compassionate desire not to "blame the victim"' (2000, p. 334).

> *In our Liverpool home*
> *Sent here from Lambeth and Rome*
> *We're better together in protest and prayer*
> *We've shouted for jobs in a voice loud and clear*
> *When the region needs allies we're proud to be here,*
> *In our Liverpool home.*
>
> Archbishop Derek Worlock

These are very reasonable reservations and raise questions that are relevant in a number of situations. And yet, and yet ... (to echo Longley). Without denying that there will be wrongs on both sides, some occasions call for partisanship. Even though some of the earthiness of small 'p' politics will rub off, staying wholly above the fray is not always an option – and certainly not an option for the poor. One way of assessing where to stand is to analyse where power lies and pose the familiar 'social justice' questions: Who wins? Who loses? Who decides? These questions can similarly relate to reflections on urban and rural areas: Whose place is it? Who owns it? Who is kept out or marginalized? Who is not made to feel at home? (Sheldrake 2001, p. 163).

## Asking awkward questions

Some Christian bodies are posing precisely these questions by observing trends and the impact of public policy especially on the most vulnerable groups. Church Action on Poverty works with church and community groups across the UK to make tackling poverty a priority: bringing home the reality of poverty; enabling

107

people in poverty to speak for themselves; working for policies to eradicate it; promoting reflection on and action for social justice. CAP would count its authority as deriving from speaking *with* not just *for* people in poverty. Digging beneath the surface of major issues, it combines an advocacy role with active involvement in running grassroots projects. It identifies problems unequivocally but is still prepared to enter the less pristine, more uncertain territory of working with others to find solutions. Striking the right balance is always difficult. How 'respectable' should CAP be? Is there a trade-off between being an accepted voice and resource for the churches and others and retaining a cutting edge? In its early life there were discussions in the national executive about whether a more appropriate name would be Church Action on Wealth. Behind this debate was the question, 'Are we sufficiently disturbing the comfortable?' In Tony Benn's words, the question 'Why are the rich rich?' may be a more telling and relevant one than 'Why are the poor poor?'

> *The myths exposed in this report, reinforced by politicians and the media, are convenient because they allow the poor to be blamed for their poverty, and the rest of society to avoid taking any of the responsibility. Myths hide the complexity of the true nature of poverty in the UK. They enable dangerous policies to be imposed on whole sections of society without their full consequences being properly examined.*
>
> JPIT 2013

The strapline of the Joint Public Issues Team (JPIT) is 'to live out the Gospel of Christ in church and society'. It helps the four churches work together on issues of justice and equality and challenge the terms in which contemporary political discourse is framed. The team produce responses to public consultations, policy briefings and reports, and study and worship resources.

Perpetuating myths about people in poverty is a frequent device to protect us from seeing our own involvement. There is often a mismatch between rhetoric and reality, and unfortunately 'majorities of British voters over several generations have been more impressed by rhetoric than reality' (King 2015, p. 132). *Truth and Lies about Poverty*, published in 2013, set out to explode such myths. As it says,

> In 1753 John Wesley said, 'So wickedly, devilishly false is that common objection, "They are poor, only because they are idle"'. Yet today church-goers and the general public alike are willing to believe that the key factors driving poverty in the UK are the personal failings of the poor – especially 'idleness'. (JPIT 2013, p. 4)

Since then, among other issues JPIT has worked on food poverty, co-producing the report with Church Action on Poverty (CAP), and on benefit sanctions, again with CAP and also the Church in Wales.

Housing Justice is another organization that combines campaigning with practical action. In the belief that human dignity is undermined by the lack of decent housing, it is the national voice of Christian action in the field of housing and homelessness.

Housing Justice supports night shelters, drop-ins and hundreds of projects nationwide. It provides training for churches and other groups who work with homeless people. It also facilitates a range of forums to enable people to voice their concerns and have their opinions heard: 'We work to unite Christians and churches of all denominations across the country to work for change. We embrace partnerships with people of all faiths (and none) who share our values of social justice and compassion' (Housing Justice, undated).

## Shared goals

On many issues Christians will find themselves in tune with people of other faiths and none. In a plural society, partnership, reconciliation and connecting with other faith traditions, narratives and communities become more important. Here are two examples, one global, the other national.

In March 2014 the issue of slavery brought leaders of all the major faiths together at the Vatican. This was less than a year after Archbishop Justin Welby visited Pope Francis and they agreed about the challenge of human trafficking as an issue for the churches. On the World Day for the Abolition of Slavery, Catholic, Anglican, Muslim, Hindu, Buddhist, Jewish and Orthodox leaders signed a joint declaration seeking the eradication of slavery and human trafficking by 2020. This agreement inaugurated the Global Freedom Network. Despite the efforts of many, human slavery is a plague on a vast scale in many countries across the world today. Victims are hidden away in places of prostitution, private homes, illegal establishments, factories, on farms, behind closed doors – and other places in the cities, villages and slums of the world's richest and poorest nations. Rather than improving, this situation is, on the contrary, probably deteriorating – nearly 36 million people are estimated to be enslaved (Global Slavery Index, undated).

'Citizens UK organizes communities to act together for power, social justice and the common good' (Citizens UK, undated). Citizens UK has chapters in various parts of the country. It is an alliance of faith communities, schools, unions and voluntary organizations reaching about half a million people. One of its campaigns, the UK Living Wage Campaign, was launched in 2001 by London Citizens' members who found that in minimum-wage jobs they struggled to make ends meet and that family and community life were squeezed. It exemplifies faith groups coming together with businesses and campaigners to find practical solutions to working poverty, and has now become a national movement.

## Grief and newness

This chapter has talked about the importance of understanding and responding to the context in which God has placed us, and has illustrated a few of the many ways we might articulate our concerns and values. It has underlined that even among Christians there will be multiple viewpoints – whether about current 'facts' or desirable future scenarios. As stated in *Who is my Neighbour?*:

> Looked at through the prism of Christian theology, the state of the world today reflects the fact that we live 'between the times' – in a world where the Holy Spirit is alive and active, yet a world still characterized by the persistence of sin. Because grace and sin are in tension for everyone, claims to have grasped ultimate truth for all time, whether in theology, politics, economics or anything else, are bound to be wrong. (Church of England 2015)

Nevertheless, without claiming superior knowledge we are obliged to engage constructively – wrestle – with the sorts of questions that are the stuff of politics and to think about whatever is true, honourable, pure, pleasing and commendable (Philippians 4.8).

The Beatitudes (Matthew 5.1–12) draw a contrast between present conditions and the future when God's kingdom is fulfilled. But the good news of Jesus is not just a future promise, it is an invitation now. The kingdom breaks in on the present – what characterizes it is its reversal of the world's values. To see the present world through God's eyes is to grieve over it. Entering into God's vision unlocks the way to newness, to a restoration of right relationships, to the fulfilment, consolation and comradeship of God's kingdom. This is prophetic ministry. It is not a once-for-all transformation, rather an ongoing process with grief and newness always interlocked. It does not come cheaply but nor is it just concerned with the big issues of the day or solely a process for 'special' people. God's concern for justice is discernible in every aspect of how we live together. Whatever our situation, the calling for us all is to be salt and light (Matthew 5.13–16). The world's discomfiting reality is the atmosphere we live and breathe; but through Christ's life, death and resurrection we also breathe new life.

# 7
# Doing Justice to Our Faith?

*Being Church means being God's people, in accordance with the great plan of his fatherly love. This means that we are to be God's leaven in the midst of humanity ... The Church must be a place of mercy, freely given, where everyone can feel welcomed, loved, forgiven and encouraged to live the good life of the Gospel.*

Pope Francis 2013, paragraph 114

This final chapter reiterates various arguments that have threaded through the book and poses some of the associated questions – ones I have set out to identify rather than answer! My hope is that the book's focus will have served to affirm Christians involved in social action and that the questions raised will provide ongoing food for thought and constructive themes for further exploration and discussion.

## A servant Church

Like other civil society organizations, the Church is distinct from the state and the market, and like them, it can encompass individual acts of kindness and charitable giving, volunteering and service to local communities. But for church members it goes further. This alertness to the needs of neighbours is part of the DNA of being a Christian. Anthony Dyson talked about the Christian task of searching for, holding to, living and struggling in the creative centre of culture. This creative centre is not an artistic conception nor is it a geographical location, rather it is to be found at 'those critical points in society where God's creativity and redemptive acts are contending with forces of meaninglessness, dispersion, disorder and despair' (Dyson 1985, p. 16).

Growth is a major preoccupation across Christian churches nowadays, driven by internal anxieties as well as by Jesus' directive to the disciples to go and make disciples of all nations (Matthew 28.19). A number of initiatives are being mounted to address numerical decline, but there is also a danger that thinking about growth and thinking about social outreach are put in quite separate compartments. When this is the case it tends to reflect a very defensive, insular attitude to growth, a preoccupation with institutional issues and a 'must try harder' approach. Yet new questions are being asked of the Church and the old answers will not suffice. In W. C. Bateman's words, 'If you keep on doing what you've always done, you'll keep on getting what you've always got.'

Christianity is an historical religion in two senses. It is based on an historical person to whom Christians must remain faithful *and* it exists as an historical entity that must adapt to its social context to retain its meaning, relevance and vitality. The point of being a Christian is not to escape from our circumstances – whatever they are – but to find God in them and find what God intended for us in them. The distinctiveness of the Christian faith lies in the 'incarnation', the complete identification of God through Christ with humanity. Embodying this in the Church means being community-centred rather than congregation-centred; recognizing and responding to the reality of people's lives: their homes and households, their neighbourhoods and wider networks, the issues they grapple with and the skills and qualities they have to give. The attractiveness of the gospel is that it is good news to the poor, whether our poverty is material or spiritual. The challenge is how to express our experience of Christ in our own concrete situation. Meeting this challenge is key to enlarging the Church's reach.

## Context is key

The importance of context has been emphasized in various ways throughout this book. Theology in any age has to achieve the right tension between the biblical message and current ways of thinking: between the universal and the particular; the transcendent and the historical. As well as being an expression of faith, theology needs to combine with other disciplines to read the style of a culture or 'trace God's hand' in the events of our time. As Malcolm Brown puts it, 'the Church's social witness must be theologically articulate and not merely a visceral reaction to pastoral problems' (2014, p. 21). We all need to think about what is unique and special about our time and place so that we can better explore our faith and better understand ourselves and how we relate to others. Where and when we live will intimately affect how we understand the gospel. Conversely, *forming* our time and place ought to be a central task of our discipleship.

When we think about place we are thinking of more than its physical features. Philip Sheldrake, in *Spaces for the Sacred*, distinguishes between space and place. The idea of place is not confined to a geographical location, rather it also links the human story in that location so that it brings together memory and human identity. This is perhaps very obvious in relation to villages. We may think of cities as more anonymous yet they are also critical to our story and to our formation and identity. Cities and urban conurbations are the best of places and the worst of places. They express human creativity and love but they are also places of injustice and inhumanity. They bring us face to face with inequalities of wealth and power and with unjust structures.

As a corporate expression of human self-definition, the city as a whole is a statement about the boundaries and potential of what it is to be human. 'What does it mean to be humane as well as human? What does human community amount to?' (Sheldrake 2001, p. 166)

The trends identified earlier have raised many questions about citizenship, the limits of the market, the role of the state and the place of regulation.

- A shrinking world with such contrasts in consumption and the use of and access to resources reframes the question 'Who is my neighbour?' It shows up in stark relief the implications of my lifestyle here in the UK for the resources, the climate and the economic well-being of those in poorer countries across the world. At the root of poverty, wherever it is found, is lack of power. Not only is there a glaring inequality of power between nations, this is strikingly apparent at individual level. For many of us living in richer countries, acting as a good neighbour in this context must cause us to examine the way we live and engage us as consumers as well lead us to challenge inequality and discriminatory practices.
- The poverty in our midst is reflected in paucity of income, housing, health and educational attainment. Medical advances open up far more possibilities in health care. Increasing health and social care demands are a feature of our ageing society. To sustain a welfare society means facing hard questions about the allocation of resources, the role of taxation and the balance of rights and responsibilities.
- Our more obviously plural society prompts the question of how we combine respect for different identities, cultures, faith traditions and forms of family life with identifying and defining human rights and expectations of citizenship. Asserting the principle of equality is a start but not the whole story. The real dilemmas are about *how* to embody equal

treatment in public policies and how to strike a balance with other policy principles (Chaplin 2011, p. 40)

- How do we counter the widespread disillusion with politics – representative and participative, local and national – and the failure of trust affecting institutions of all kinds: corporations, companies, banks, the media and not excluding the Church?

## Questions for activists

More day-to-day questions hover in the background of a lot of the choices we make consciously or unconsciously, especially in relation to the more organized forms of social action.

- How far does involvement risk embracing the 'wrong' goals – being co-opted into accounting, public relations and marketing language, output measures and metrics and losing our grip on compassion, social justice and equality?
- In part this is asking about the level of pragmatism – or do we call it compromise? – that we accept. Life is full of trade-offs, even though these may be most obvious in, for example, politics. If political realism is the art of the possible, how do we distinguish the possible and principled from the expedient?
- Another dimension of this question is: How far is involvement a precondition of 'reading the signs of the times' or something that precludes it because we are so involved that we can't see the wood for the trees or are too close to power and too understanding of all the ifs and buts and maybes?
- How do we set priorities? For example, are there instances of special pleading for institutional interests that disable our ability to speak about wider issues?
- How far do we stick to ideals about behaviour and relationships at the expense of responding to a rather messier reality and people's needs arising out of that reality?

- How do we deal with sin? Those of us involved in social responsibility/justice and peace organizations tend to restrict ourselves to structural sin. We can risk so stressing issues of economic and social structures and the distribution of power that we skate round questions of personal responsibility, particularly among those we see as victims. They may well be victims but we do them no service by assuming they are helpless.

- Conversely we can fall into the trap of forgetting that those who operate the 'system' are human beings and that the concept of human dignity embraces them as much as others.

- How do we define our Christian identity and delineate what is essentially Christian? And how do we do this while avoiding fundamentalism and division and leaving open channels for dialogue and negotiating difference, whether with other Christians or people of other faiths and none?

## Being present – enduring and faithful

[T]he very idea of a 'common' good implies that such a good can only be identified when all members of a community have been given space to testify to their own experiences, struggles and insights. (Jonathan Chaplin, in Sagovsky and McGrail 2015, p. 106)

After defining the Christian task at the creative centre of culture, Anthony Dyson went on to say that the common Christian calling is 'to be and to persist, to bear portions of the world's sufferings, to fall and to be picked up, to seek to be "salt" and "light" at these points, in the day to day fabric of our human lives' (Dyson 1985, p. 16). The *common* Christian calling – it is not the prerogative of laity or clergy or any particular denomination or

Christian tradition. And if we have to be inclusive in our action we must also be inclusive in our conversation. One step on the road will be arenas in which people of widely differing interests and perspectives can come together, putting aside their tribal loyalties or party-political affiliations, and where all voices are given a respectful hearing – within the Christian community and in wider society. This book originated from the Together for the Common Good initiative. T4CG endeavours to create such spaces for conversations, to form stepping stones to action and to promote a growing movement of people united in seeking the common good. Perhaps, like happiness (according to graffiti that I frequently pass), the common good is not a destination but a journey – and a journey made more daunting, exciting and fulfilling by the company we keep.

*A footnote*: I recently came across this hymn about Josephine Butler, the Christian nineteenth-century social reformer who challenged the inconsistent and hypocritical standards of her time – which unjustly disadvantaged women – and worked for legislative reform to provide them with some degree of protection, equality and justice. In just a few lines it captures the themes of this book in a story of personal discipleship, illustrated in her life of prayer and civic involvement, social action and speaking out.

> For God's sake let us dare
> To pray like Josephine,
> Who felt with Christ the world's despair
> And asked what love could mean.
>
> He was her truth, her way,
> Through him he spoke again
> For each exploited Maggie May
> Each modern Magdalen.

She forced her age to face
What most it feared to see,
The double standards at the base
Of its prosperity.

Grant us, like her, no rest
In systems which degrade
At once oppressors and oppressed,
By grace for glory made.

Elizabeth Cosnett

# Bibliography

Atherton, John, 2000, *Public Theology for Changing Times*, London: SPCK.

Atherton, John, Baker, Chris and Reader, John, 2011, *Christianity and the New Social Order: A Manifesto for a Fairer Future*, London: SPCK.

Atkinson, Anthony, 2015, *Inequality: What Can be Done?*, Cambridge, MA: Harvard University Press.

Baker, Chris and Skinner, Hannah, 2006, *Faith in Action: The Dynamic Connection between Spiritual and Religious Capital*, Manchester: William Temple Foundation.

Baker, Chris, 2007, 'Religious Literacy, Faithful Capital and Language', ESRC Seminar paper, Cambridge: Anglia Ruskin University, 23 January.

Baker, Chris and Miles-Watson, Jonathan, 2007, *Faith and Traditional Capitals: Defining the Public Scope of Religious Capital*, Manchester: William Temple Foundation.

Barrett, Clive (ed.), 2012, *Unity in Process: Reflections on Ecumenism*, London: Darton, Longman & Todd.

Battle, John, undated, 'Praying with the Poor' – www.catholicsocialteaching.org.uk/themes/solidarity/reflection/praying-poor.

Bauman, Zygmunt, 2000, *Liquid Modernity*, Cambridge: Polity Press.

Bell, G. K. A., 1954, *The Kingship of Christ*, London: Penguin Special.

Benedict XVI, 2009, *Caritas in veritate*.

Bennett, Katy, Beynon, Huw and Hudson, Ray, 2000, *Coalfields Regeneration: Dealing with the Consequences of Industrial Decline*, York: Joseph Rowntree Foundation.

Brown, Malcolm (ed.), 2014, *Anglican Social Theology*, London: Church House Publishing.

Capron, Lucy and Ayre, David, 2015, *The Wolf at the Door: How Council Tax Debt Collection is Harming Children*, London: The Children's Society.

Catholic Bishops' Conference of England and Wales, 1980, *The Easter People: A Message from the Roman Catholic Bishops of England and Wales in light of the National Pastoral Congress, Liverpool, 1980*, Slough: St Paul Publications.

Catholic Bishops' Conference of England and Wales, 1996, *The Common Good and the Catholic Church's Social Teaching*, Manchester: Gabriel Communications.

Catholic Bishops' Conference of England and Wales, 2001, *Vote for the Common Good* – www.catholicnews.org.uk/Catholic-News-Media-Library/Archive-Media-Assets/Files/CBCEW-Publications/Vote-for-The-Common-Good.

Centre for Catholic Studies, 'Receptive Ecumenism', undated, www.dur.ac.uk/theology.religion/ccs/projects/receptiveecumenism.

Centre for Welfare Reform – www.centreforwelfarereform.org.

Chaplin, Jonathan, 2011, *Multiculturalism: A Christian Retrieval*, London: Theos.

Church of England General Synod, 2014, *The Common Good: The Church and Politics Today*, A paper from the Mission and Public Affairs Council, GS1956, July 2014.

Church of England, 2015, *Who is my Neighbour?*, A Letter from the House of Bishops to the People and Parishes of the Church of England for the General Election, 2015.

Church Urban Fund, 2012, *Survival Strategies: A Survey of the Impact of the Current Economic Climate on Community Organisations in the most Deprived areas of England*, London: Church Urban Fund.

Church Urban Fund and Charity Evaluation Services, 2014, *Tackling Poverty Together: Impact Report of the Together Network* – www.cuf.org.uk/sites/default/files/users/Bethany Eckley/Together Network Impact Report 2014.pdf.

Church Urban Fund and the Church of England, 2015 (authored by Bethany Eckley and Tom Sefton), *Church in Action: A National Survey of Church-Based Social Action*, London: Church Urban Fund and the Church of England.

Church Urban Fund research reports – www.cuf.org.uk/research.

Citizens UK, undated – www.citizensuk.org/what_we_do.

Clarke, A., Hill, L., Marshall, B., Monk, S., Pereira, I., Thomson, E., Whithead, C. and Williams, P., 2014, *Evaluation of the Removal of the Spare Room Subsidy: Interim Report*, London: Department for Work and Pensions.

Clements, Keith, 2011, *Learning to Speak: The Church's Voice in Public Affairs*, Eugene, OR: Wipf & Stock.

Cornick, David, 2013, 'Changes in English Christianity and Changes at CTE' – www.cte.org.uk/features.

Davey, Andrew, 2007, 'Faithful Cities: Locating Everyday Faithfulness', *Contact: Practical Theology and Pastoral Care* 152, pp. 8–20.

Demant, V. A., 1952, *Religion and the Decline of Capitalism*, London: Faber & Faber.

Department for Environment, Food & Rural Affairs (Defra), 2013, 'Statistical Digest of Rural England' www.gov.uk/government/statistics/statistical-digest-of-rural-england-2013.

Department of Communities and Local Government, 2015, Housing Statistical Release, June.

Dyson, Anthony, 1985, 'Clericalism, Church and Laity', in *All Are Called: Towards a Theology of the Laity*, Essays from a Working Party of the General Synod Board of Education under the Chairmanship of the Bishop of Oxford, London: CIO Publishing, pp. 13–17.

*Faith in England's Northwest: The Contribution made by Faith Communities to Civil Society in the Region*, 2003, Northwest Development Agency.

*Faith in England's Northwest: How Faith Communities Contribute to Social and Economic Wellbeing*, 2009, Northwest Development Agency.

*Faith in the City: A Call for Action by Church and Nation*, 1985, The Report of the Archbishop of Canterbury's Commission on Urban Priority Areas, London: Church House Publishing.

*Faithful Cities: A Call for Celebration, Vision and Justice*, 2006, The Report of the Commission on Life and Faith, London: Church House Publishing and Methodist Publishing House.

Forrester, Duncan B., 1989, *Beliefs, Values and Policies: Conviction Politics in a Secular Age*, Oxford: Oxford University Press.

Furnival, John and Knowles, Ann, 1998, *Archbishop Derek Worlock: His Personal Journey*, London: Geoffrey Chapman.

*Gaudium et spes*, Pastoral Constitution on the Church in the Modern World, promulgated by His Holiness Pope Paul VI on December 7, 1965 – www.vatican.va/archive/hist_councils/ii_vatican_council/documents/vat-ii_const_19651207_gaudium-et-spes_en.html.

Giddens, Anthony, 1998, *The Third Way*, Cambridge: Polity Press.

Giddens, Anthony, 1999, *Runaway World: How Globalisation is Reshaping our Lives*, London: Profile Books.

Global Slavery Index, undated – www.globalslaveryindex.org/findings.

*Growing Together: A Social Understanding of Church Growth*, 2014, Council for Social Responsibility, Anglican Diocese of Portsmouth – www.csrnet.org.uk.

Gutiérrez, Gustavo, 2010, *A Theology of Liberation*, London: SCM Press.

Heath, Sarah, 2014, *Housing Demand and Need (England)*, Standard Note SNO6921, for the House of Commons Library – see http://researchbriefings.parliament.uk/ResearchBriefing/Summary/SN06921#fullreport.

Hope+ Foodbank, undated – www.liverpoolcathedral.org.uk/about/foodbank-hope.aspx.

Housing Justice, undated – www.housingjustice.org.uk/pages/what-we-do.html.

Hume, Basil, 1996, Preface, in Catholic Bishops' Conference of England and Wales, *The Common Good and the Catholic Church's Social Teaching*.

*Inequality and Financialisation: A Dangerous Mix*, 2014, New Economics Foundation and Friedrich-Ebert-Stiftung, December.

Innes, David and Tetlow, Gemma, 2015, *Central Cuts, Local Decision-Making: Changes in Local Government Spending and Revenues in England, 2009–10 to 2014–15*, London: Institute for Fiscal Studies.

Ivereigh, A., 2014, *The Great Reformer: Francis and the Making of a Radical Pope*, London: Allen & Unwin.

Jackson, Tim, 2009, *Prosperity without Growth: Economics for a Finite Planet*, London: Earthscan.

John Paul II, 1987, *Sollicitudo rei socialis*.

John Paul II, 1999, 'Respect for Human Rights: The Secret of True Peace', Message for the Celebration of the World Day of Peace.

Joint Public Issues Team (JPIT), 2013, *The Lies We Tell Ourselves: Ending Comfortable Myths about Poverty*, the Baptist Union of Great Britain, the Methodist Church and the United Reformed Church – www.jointpublicissues.org.uk/truthandliesaboutpoverty.

Joint Public Issues Team (JPIT) and Church Action on Poverty (CAP), 2014, *Faith in Foodbanks? Resources for Churches*, the Baptist Union of Great Britain, the Methodist Church, the United Reformed Church and Church Action on Poverty – www.jointpublicissues.org.uk/faithinfoodbanks.

Joseph Rowntree Foundation, 2014, 'Poverty Rate by Ethnicity' – http://data.jrf.org.uk/data/poverty-rate-ethnicity.

Joseph Rowntree Foundation, 2015, 'Fuel Poverty in England' – http://data.jrf.org.uk/data/fuel-poverty-england.

Kairos Theologians, 1985, *Challenge to the Church: The Kairos Document – A Theological Comment on the Crisis in South Africa* – http://ujamaa.ukzn.ac.za/Libraries/manuals/The_Kairos_Documents.sflb.ashx.

Kelly, Kevin, 2012, *50 Years Receiving Vatican II: A Personal Odyssey*, Dublin: The Columba Press.

King, Anthony, 2015, *Who Governs Britain?*, London: Pelican.

Layard, Richard, 2006, *Happiness: Lessons from a New Science*, London: Penguin Books.

*live*simply, undated – www.catholicsocialteaching.org.uk/resources/about/#about; and www.catholicsocialteaching.org.uk/terms-conditions.

Longley, Clifford, 2000, *The Worlock Archive*, London: Geoffrey Chapman.

McInnes, Tom, Aldridge, Hannah, Bushe, Sabrina, Tinson, Adam and Born, Theo Barry, *Monitoring Poverty and Social Exclusion 2014*, Joseph Rowntree Foundation and New Policy Institute, 2014.

Marquand, Judith, 2013, 'Why I Left the Civil Service: Thatcher, Trust and Democracy' – www.opendemocracy.net, 17 April.

Marsh, Colin and Currin, Jim, 2013, *Mission-shaped Unity: Missio Dei and a New Way of Being Churches Together*, Ev103, Cambridge: Grove Books.

May, Don and Simey, Margaret, 1989, 'The Servant Church in Granby', in *Cross Connections*, occasional papers on Church and Society, ed. Hilary Russell, Merseyside Churches' Urban Institute and Centre for Urban Studies, University of Liverpool. See http://togetherforthecommongood.co.uk/case-studies/articles/the-servant-church-in-granby.html.

Methodist Church, undated – www.methodist.org.uk/who-we-are/relationships-with-other-denominations/ecumenism-in-britain-and-ireland/england/resources/ecumenical-basics/guidance-notes/the-c-scale-of-relationships.

Money Advice Trust, 2014, *Changing Household Budgets* – www.infohub.moneyadvicetrust.org/content_files/files/changing_household_budgets_report_final.pdf.

New Economics Foundation – www.neweconomics.org/blog/by/environment.

Office for National Statistics, 2015, 'Persistent Poverty in the UK and EU, 2008–2013' – www.ons.gov.uk/ons/dcp171776_403629.pdf.

O'Neill, Onora, 2002, *A Question of Trust*, The BBC Reith Lectures 2002, Cambridge: Cambridge University Press.

Oxfam, 2014, *Even It Up: Time to End Extreme Inequality*, Oxford: Oxfam.

Parkinson, Michael, 1985, *Liverpool on the Brink*, Berkshire: Policy Journals.

Pohl, Christine D., 1999, *Making Room: Recovering Hospitality as a Christian Tradition*, Grand Rapids: Eerdmans.

Pope Francis, 2013, *Evangelii Gaudium: The Joy of the Gospel*, London: Catholic Truth Society.

Pope Francis, 1 January 2014, 'Fraternity, the Foundational Pathway to Peace', Message for the Celebration of the World Day of Peace.

*Populorum Progressio – On the Development of Peoples*, 1967, Encyclical Letter of Pope Paul VI, March 1967 – www.papalencyclicals.net/Paul06/p6develo.htm.

Preston, Ronald H., 1994, *Confusions in Christian Social Ethics: Problems for Geneva and Rome*, London: SCM Press.

Probert, Susan, Bonner, Adam and Chapman, Daniel, undated, *Keeping the Faith: Retaining Christian Distinctiveness in Your Community Project*, London: Church Urban Fund and Liveability.

Putnam, Robert D., 2000, *Bowling Alone: The Collapse and Revival of American Community*, New York: Touchstone, Simon & Schuster.

PWC, 2015, *Precious Plastic 2015: How Britons Fell Back in Love with Borrowing*.

Ralph, Nick, 2015, *Growing Together: A Social Understanding of Church Growth*, Council for Social Responsibility, Diocese of Portsmouth – www.csrnet.org.uk.

Russell, Hilary (ed.), 1989, 'The Birds Eye Debate', in *Cross Connections*, occasional papers on Church and Society, Merseyside Churches' Urban Institute and Centre for Urban Studies, University of Liverpool.

Russell, Hilary, 1995, *Poverty Close to Home: A Christian Understanding*, London: Mowbray.

Russell, Hilary, 2012, *Resourcing Christian Community Action: Parishes and Partnerships* – www.churchofengland.org/how2help.

Sacks, Jonathan, 2001, *The Dignity of Difference: How to Avoid the Clash of Civilizations*, London: Continuum.

Sagovsky, N. and McGrail, P. (eds), 2015, *Together for the Common Good: Towards a National Conversation*, London: SCM Press.

Schreiter, Robert J., 1985, *Constructing Local Theologies*, London: SCM Press.

Selby, Peter, 1991, *Belonging: Challenge to a Tribal Church*, London: SPCK.

Sennett, Richard, 2003, *Respect: The Formation of Character in an Age of Inequality*, London: Allen Lane.

Sheldrake, Philip, 2001, *Spaces for the Sacred*, London: SCM Press.

Sheppard, David, 1974, *Built as a City: God and the Urban World Today*, London: Hodder & Stoughton.

Sheppard, David, 1983, *Bias to the Poor*, London: Hodder & Stoughton.

Sheppard, David and Worlock, Derek, 1988, *Better Together*, London: Hodder & Stoughton.

Sheppard, David and Worlock, Derek, 1994, *With Hope in Our Hearts*, London: Hodder & Stoughton.

Sheppard, David, 2002, *Steps Along Hope Street*, London: Hodder & Stoughton.

Shilson-Thomas, Annabel (ed.), 2008, *Live*simply, London: CAFOD.

Smith, Austin, 1990, *Journeying with God: Paradigms of Power and Powerlessness*, London: Sheed & Ward.

Smith, Greg (ed.), 2015a, *Reflections on Research by the Evangelical Alliance*, London: Evangelical Alliance.

Smith, Greg, 2015b, *Progressive Localism and the Hole(e)y Safety Net*, Temple Tracts: Issue 1, Volume 1 – www.williamtemplefoundation.org.uk.

Smith, Noel, Davis, Abigail and Hirsch, Donald, 2010, *A Minimum Income Standard for Rural Areas*, York: Joseph Rowntree Foundation.

Sykes, Stephen, 1983, *Christian Theology Today*, London: Mowbray.

Tanner, Mary, 2013, paper at session 'Better Together Today: Sharing "Common Good" Language' at Together for the Common Good, conference 6–8 September 2013 entitled 'Understanding How Faith-Based Collaboration can Work Best for the Common Good' – http://togetherforthecommongood.co.uk/files/images/conference speakers texts/T4CG MARY TANNER delivered FINAL.pdf.

Temple, William, 1942, *Christianity and Social Order*, Harmondsworth: Penguin.

Temple, William, 1958, *Religious Experience and Other Essays and Addresses*, collected and edited by A. E. Baker, Cambridge: Lutterworth Press.

Together Middlesbrough, 2013, *Faith in Action: A Survey of Christian Social Action around Middlesbrough*.

Townsend, Peter, 1979, *Poverty in the United Kingdom*, London: Allen Lane.

*Unemployment and the Future of Work*, 1997, An Enquiry for the Churches, London: CCBI.

UNHCR, 2014, 'The Facts: Asylum in the UK' – www.unhcr.org.uk/about-us/the-uk-and-asylum.html.

United States Conference of Catholic Bishops, 1986, *Economic Justice for All: Pastoral Letter on Catholic Social Teaching and the U.S. Economy* – www.usccb.org/upload/economic_justice_for_all.pdf.

Visser 't Hooft, W. A. and Oldham, J. H., 1937, *The Church and its Function in Society*, London: Allen & Unwin.

Wallis, Jim, 2013, *On God's Side: What Religion Forgets and Politics asn't Learned about Serving the Common Good*, Grand Rapids: Brazos Press.

Welby, Justin, 2014, 'Archbishop of Canterbury's Message to the Third International Receptive Ecumenism Conference, Fairfield University, Connecticut, USA, 9–12 June 2014' – www.churchofengland.org/media/2006001/receptive%20ecumenism%20conf%20abc%20message%2013%205%202014.pdf.

Wilkinson, Richard and Pickett, Kate, 2010, *The Spirit Level: Why Equality is Better for Everyone*, Harmondsworth: Penguin Books.

Williams, Rowan, 2004, Keynote address to Mission-Shaped Church Conference, 23 June 2004.

Williams, Rowan, 2007, *Christianity, Public Religion and the Common Good*, a lecture given at St Andrew's Cathedral, Singapore, 12 May 2007.

Williams, Rowan, 2008, *From Welfare State to Welfare Society: The Contribution of Faiths to Happiness and Wellbeing in a Plural Civil Society*, Archbishop's lecture celebrating the 60th anniversary of the William Temple Foundation, Manchester, 5 November 2008.

Williams, Rowan, 2012, *Faith in the Public Square*, London: Bloomsbury/Continuum.

World Council of Churches, 1982, *Baptism, Eucharist and Ministry*, Geneva: WCC.

World Council of Churches, 2012, *The Church: Towards a Common Vision*.

Wyler, Steve (Locality), de Groot, Lucy (CSV), Slocock, Caroline (Civil Exchange), Irwin, Joe (National Association of Voluntary and Community Action) and Wookey, Charles (Catholic Bishops Conference of England and Wales), 2013, *Call to*

*Action for the Common Good*, Research and report funded by the Carnegie Trust.

Wyler, S., 2014, 'The Common Good Must be at the Heart of Charitable Mission', in *Making Good: The Future of the Voluntary Sector*, edited by C. Slocock, London: Civil Exchange.

# Index